The Congregational Minute

by

Robert Hellam

Robert Hellam, Publisher
Seaside, California

Dedicated to my dear wife, Connie

Hellam, Robert
The Congregational Minute

Introduction

This book is a collection of talks given at the Church of the Oaks, Del Rey Oaks, California, during the Sunday worship service, from May 2010 through January 2012. (Due to my occasional absence or to time constraints, there was not a "Congregational Minute" during every single one of those weeks.) We liked the title "The Congregational Minute," even though one of our members joked that the talks ought to be titled "The Congregational Five Minutes."

These talks began when the moderator and other members of our church's Executive Council expressed the opinion that most of our members really did not know a lot about the Congregational Way. So this series is designed as an introductory course into our Congregational history and polity.

Every effort has been made to ensure that the facts presented here are supported by reliable sources. (These pieces were originally written with no thought of publication, so in some cases I did not remember the original sources consulted, and the footnotes might reflect other sources that contain the same information.) Quotations will be cited, but facts are not annotated when they are generally agreed upon by all or most of the sources consulted. When opinions are expressed, they are not necessarily the opinions of Church of the Oaks or of the National Association of Congregational Christian Churches.

Contents

May 16, 2010
Congregational Beginnings

Harry Butman, one of the founders of our association and also one of our foremost historians, claims that Congregationalism began as early as the fourteenth century with the Lollards, followers of John Wycliffe, the famous translator of the Bible into English who is often called "The Morning Star of the Reformation." But Dr. Butman concedes that most historians do not agree with him on this point.[1] He goes on to say, "Some authorities say that the Plumbers' Hall Society [also called the Bridewell Privy Church] was the first Congregational Church."[2] John Waddington, another historian, says, "The first Congregational Church in the reign of Elizabeth [I] was formed in 1567, by a company of Christian people in the Bridewell [district] of the City of London, by Mr. Richard Fitz." He continues, "The privations they endured in prison, with the death of their pastor and deacon, made no change in their convictions, or in their purpose to maintain them under all conditions. Immediately, therefore, on their liberation from bonds, they resumed their meetings in Whitechapel Street."[3]

What was the charge against these people? Historian Richard Dixon says that, according to the Bishop of London, it was "that they not only absented themselves from their parish churches and other assemblies of obedient Christians in the realm, but also made assemblies and gatherings, using prayer and preachings, and ministering the Sacraments among

---

[1] Harry R. Butman, *The Lord's Free People* (Oak Creek: Congregational Press, no date), 17.

[2] Butman, *Symbols of Our Way* (Oak Creek: Congregational Press, no date), 3.

[3] John Waddington, *Congregational History, 1700-1800* (London: Longmans, Green, and Co., 1874), on unpaginated Website «http://www.ebooksread.com/authors-eng/john-waddington/congregational-history-1700-1800-in-relation-to-contemporaneous-events-educat-hci/1-congregational-history-1700-1800-in-relation-to-contemporaneous-events-educat-hci.shtml» (accessed 23 Apr 2012).

themselves."[4]   In other words, they did not follow the practices of the established Church of England, which the British government wanted all people to follow for the sake of national unity. So in the view of the church-state establishment, these people were not only heretics but traitors.

While they were still in prison, they composed their church order, which was titled "The True Marks of Christ's Church." Harry Butman very movingly calls this document a "cry from the dungeon."[5] Butman talks about another early Congregational document as "a yell of rage, a cry in the night, a lament for the death of those whose only offense was their faith, for the old and sick taken out of prison a few hours before the end and left to die on the sidewalk. . . . These dungeons must have been foul beyond belief in the cruel years when nameless Congregationalists coughed out their tubercular lungs, unjustly jailed, uneased by a doctor's skill, uncomforted by the touch of a kinsman's hand. There is a terrible reality behind the familiar declaration that our freedom is bought with blood."[6]

Here is the text of the covenant of the Bridewell church: "The order of the Privy Church in London, which by the malice of Satan, is falsely slandered and evil spoken of. The minds of them that by the strength and working of the Almighty, our Lord Jesus Christ, have set their hands and hearts to the pure, unmingled, and sincere worshiping of God, according to His blessed and glorious Word in all things only, abolishing and abhorring all traditions and inventions of man whatsoever in the same religion and service of our Lord God, knowing this always, that the true and afflicted Church of our Lord and Savior Jesus Christ either hath, or else ever more continually under the cross striveth for to have, first and foremost, the glorious Word and Evangel preached, not in bondage and subjection, but freely and purely; secondly, to have the Sacraments ministered purely only and altogether according to the institution and good Word of the Lord Jesus, without any tradition or invention of man; and last of all, to have not the filthy Canon Law,

---

[4]Richard Watson Dixon, *History of the Church of England* (Oxford: Clarendon Press, 1902), 167 «http://books.google.com/books» (accessed 23 Apr 2012).

[5]Butman, *Symbols*, 3.

[6]Butman, *Lord's Free People*, 19-20.

but discipline only and altogether agreeable to the same heavenly and almighty Word of our good Lord Jesus Christ."—Richard Fitz, Minister.[7]

John von Rohr, another Congregational historian, speaks of the church's "self-description as 'a poor congregation whom God hath separated from the Church of England and from the mingled and false worship therein.' But a new style of church organization and government also was evident, including covenant commitment by each member and the congregation's assumption of responsibility for election of its minister and discipline of its membership."[8]

---

[7]Waddington, *Congregational History 1200-1567* (London: Longmans, Green, & Co., 1869)
«http://www.archive.org/stream/congregationalhi1869wadd/congregationalhi1869wad d_djvu.txt» (accessed 24 Apr 2012).

[8]John von Rohr, *The Shaping of American Congregationalism 1620-1957* (Cleveland: The Pilgrim Press, 1992), 8.

May 23, 2010
Robert Browne

According to Harry Butman, many say that Robert Browne "was the first to gather, in Norwich in 1580, a clearly recognizable Congregational Church." This, by the way, is why early Congregationalists were often called "Brownists." Butman goes on, "Browne was an odd stick, definitely neurotic in his final days. . . . This instability has cost him the high reputation which his ideas deserve. As an old man and rector of a little Anglican Church, he was haled into court for belting the tax collector over the head with his cane. . . . In his book *Reformation without Tarrying for Any*, he declared that the magistrate—the civil power—must stay out of Church affairs. . . . Browne [also] recognized the need for [church] councils and the relationship of local Churches with each other. However unstable his personality, Robert Browne is undoubtedly the intellectual father of Congregationalism."[9]

Browne had started out as a Puritan within the Church of England, with Presbyterian leanings. Later, he became a separatist, and his congregation was persecuted by the Bishop of Norwich. According to John von Rohr, the charge that got Browne thrown into prison was that he "was encouraging worshipers to come together in private houses and conventicles, a violation of the proper ways of church assembly."[10] Browne and his congregation fled to Holland, a generation before the famous Pilgrims did the same thing. But there was a split in the congregation, and Browne took his followers to Scotland, where the Church of Scotland persecuted them as severely as had the Church of England. Eventually, Browne returned to England, renounced separatism, and died in 1633 as an Anglican priest.

While he was still a Congregationalist, Browne wrote a book in 1582 that was called *A Book Which Showeth the Life and Manners of All True Christians, and How Unlike They Are unto Turks and Papists and Heathen Folk*. This was a statement of Congregational principles, written in the form of a catechism. Following are some of the questions and answers in the book.

Wherefore are we called the people of God and Christians? *Because that by a willing Covenant made with our God, we are under the government of God and Christ, and thereby do lead a godly and Christian life.*

---

[9]Butman, *Lord's Free People*, 18.

[10]Von Rohr, 10.

How must the church be first planted and gathered under one kind of government? *First by a covenant and condition, made on God's behalf. Secondly by a covenant and condition made on our behalf. Thirdly by using the sacrament of Baptism to seal those conditions and covenants.*

What is the covenant or condition on God's behalf? *His promise to be our God and Savior, if we forsake not His government by disobedience. Also His promise to be the God of our seed, while we are his people. Also the gift of His Spirit to His children as an inward calling and furtherance of godliness.*

What is the covenant or condition on our behalf? *We must offer and give up ourselves to be of the church and people of God. We must likewise offer and give up our children and others, being under age, if they be of our household and we have full power over them. We must make profession that we are His people by submitting ourselves to His laws and government.*

How must the Word be preached? *The preacher, being called and meet thereto, must show the redemption of Christians by Christ, and the promises received by faith. . . . Also they must show the right use of that redemption, in suffering with Christ to die unto sin by repentance. Also the raising and quickening again upon repentance.*

How must [the Church] be further builded, according unto church government? *First by communion of the graces and offices in the Head of the Church, which is Christ. Secondly, by communion of the graces and offices in the body, which is the Church of Christ. Thirdly, by using the Sacrament of the Lord's Supper as a seal of this communion.*[11]

---

[11]Williston Walker, ed., *The Creeds and Platforms of Congregationalism* (New York: The Pilgrim Press, 1991), 18-21. [I have modernized the spelling in this, as well as in most of the subsequent sources that are cited in this present work.]

May 30, 2010
Barrow and Greenwood

A separatist congregation was formed in London in the mid-1580's, meeting in secret. Because they met in secret, they would have been lost to history if they had not been discovered by the authorities in 1587. The founders of the congregation were John Greenwood and Henry Barrow. Greenwood had been an Anglican priest who was expelled from the Church of England because of his Puritan beliefs. Barrow was a lawyer who had gone to hear a Puritan sermon completely out of curiosity and was converted to the Puritan way of thinking. Barrow would write later that separation from the Church of England had been necessary for four reasons: the Anglican church had *a false membership* (a mixture of believers and unbelievers), *a false ministry* (pastors chosen by bishops), *a false worship* (ritualistic worship dictated by the Book of Common Prayer), and *a false government* (the local congregation not being permitted to call its own leaders or to discipline its own membership).[12] Barrow and Greenwood were imprisoned and tortured for their beliefs, and they were finally executed by hanging. While they were in prison, a Welsh preacher named John Penry joined their congregation. He, too, was arrested and hanged.

In 1591, Francis Johnson was elected the new pastor of the London Separatists. He was a former Anglican priest who had been a Puritan but not a separatist. In fact, he had even ordered the burning of a book written by Henry Barrow. Later, however, he joined the London group. He was also imprisoned, but when he was released he resumed leadership of the congregation, which had fled to Amsterdam while he was in prison. There, Henry Ainsworth became the teaching elder of the congregation. (Johnson was the preaching elder.)

This group produced two important Congregational documents: the London Confession of 1589, called "A True Description out of the Word of God of the Visible Church"; and the Confession of 1596, printed in Amsterdam, which had a title that was about a hundred words long. The beginning words of the title were "A True Confession of the Faith and Humble Acknowledgment of the Allegiance Which We, Her Majesty's Subjects, Falsely Called Brownists, Do Hold towards God, and Yield to Her Majesty and All Others That Are over Us in the Lord."

---

[12]Von Rohr, 11.

Here are some excerpts from the London Confession: "As there is but one God and Father of all, one Lord over all, and one Spirit: so is there but one truth, one faith, one salvation, one Church, called in one hope, joined in one profession, guided by one rule, even the Word of the Most High. . . . The Church as it is universally understood containeth in it all the elect of God that have been, are, or shall be. . . . [The local church is] a company and fellowship of faithful and holy people gathered in the Name of Christ Jesus, their only King, Priest, and Prophet, worshiping Him aright, being peaceably and quietly governed by His officers and laws, keeping the unity of faith in the bond of peace and love unfeigned. . . . Here is no intrusion of climbing up another way into the sheepfold than by the holy and free election of the Lord's holy and free people. . . . Thus they orderly proceed to ordination by fasting and prayer. . . . Thus hath every one of the people interest in the election and ordination of their officers. . . ."[13]

The Confession of 1596 begins, "Thou canst not lightly be ignorant, gentle reader, what evils and afflictions, for our profession and faith towards God, we have sustained at the hands of our own nation . . . as if we were the most notorious obstinate heretics and disloyal subjects to our gracious Queen Elizabeth that are this day to be found in all the land."[14] It goes on to insist that the congregation is determined to render unto Caesar what is Caesar's, and unto God what is God's. One important plank in the Confession is its description of how a person is called to the ministry of a local church, not by a bishop but by the congregation: ". . . None may usurp or execute a ministry but such as are rightly called by the church whereof they stand ministers. . . ."[15]

---

[13]Walker, 33, 35.

[14]Ibid., 49.

[15]Ibid., 66.

June 6, 2010
Scrooby

Scrooby is a village in Nottinghamshire in England, so far north that it is almost on the Yorkshire county line. Today, it is what we Americans might call a one-horse town, with only about a tenth of the population of Del Rey Oaks, but in the sixteenth century it was an important stopping place on the Great North Road. A baby boy was born there and named after his father. Scholars give different dates for his birth, but most say that he was born in 1566. That would have made him nine years old in 1575, when his father, William Brewster, was named tavernkeeper and postmaster of the village.

The younger Brewster left home to enter Cambridge University at age seventeen. Robert Browne, whom we discussed a few weeks ago, was a student there during the same period, and he had made quite an impact among the Cambridge students. John Greenwood and John Penry, mentioned in last week's Congregational Minute, were Brewster's classmates (and so, by the way, was Christopher Marlowe). At age nineteen, Brewster became secretary to Sir William Davison, an official in Queen Elizabeth's government and a Puritan. Proving the old adage that "no good deed shall go unpunished," Elizabeth had Davison sign the death warrant for Mary Queen of Scots, and afterward sentenced him to prison for the deed. So Brewster's employment ended there, but when his father died in 1590 he himself was appointed postmaster at Scrooby.[16]

In the nearby village of Gainsborough was a Separatist congregation led by John Smyth. It grew so quickly that it split off another congregation that began meeting in Brewster's home under Pastor Richard Clyfton. Soon a former Anglican priest named John Robinson became the teaching elder at Scrooby, and one of his first acts as pastor was to lead the church in drafting a covenant in 1606. Some of the words of that covenant will sound very familiar to us: they promised the Lord "to walk in all His ways, made known or to be made known unto them, according to their best endeavors, whatever it should cost them."[17] Before long the little church was publicly denouncing

---

[16]Esther H. Lindsey, *Signers of the Compact Who Left Descendants* (Carmel: Monterey Bay Colony, Society of Mayflower Descendants in the State of California, 1996), 10-11.

[17]Von Rohr, 16.

what they called the "base and beggarly ceremonies" of the Church of England, proclaiming that "the lordly and tyrannous power of the prelates ought not to be submitted unto," for "bishops and elders are not lords over God's creation, as if the Church could not *be* without them."[18] Nothing ought to be done in a local church without the consent of the congregation. The Archbishop of York caught wind of this dangerous doctrine, and soon, like other Congregationalists before them, the Scrooby congregation was being harassed by the authorities.

In 1607, most of the congregation spent almost all their money for passage on a ship to the Netherlands. They went to the port of Boston, in Lincolnshire, and oversaw the loading of their possessions on board the ship. The story continues in the words of William Bradford: "And when [the ship's captain] had them and their goods aboard, he betrayed them, having beforehand plotted with [government officials] so to do; who took them and put them into open boats, and there rifled and ransacked them, searching them to their shirts for money, yea, even the women, further than became modesty; and then carried them back into the town, and made them a spectacle and wonderment to the multitude, which came flocking on all sides to behold them. Being thus . . . rifled and stripped of their money, books and much other goods, they were presented to the magistrates. . . ."[19] They were all imprisoned for a month, and most of them were then released, but seven of the leaders remained in prison.

A year later, in 1608, the congregation successfully emigrated to Holland, although the authorities came just as the ship was leaving and before all could board. Before too long, though, all were united in Amsterdam with John Smyth. A year later, Smyth and Clyfton had differences and split the congregation, and John Robinson led a third group to the city of Leiden. By

---

[18]George F. Willison, *Saints and Strangers: Being the Lives of the Pilgrim Fathers & Their Families, with Their Friends & Foes; & an Account of Their Posthumous Wanderings in Limbo, Their Final Resurrection & Rise to Glory, & the Strange Pilgrimages of Plymouth Rock* (New York: Reynal & Hitchcock, 1945), 53.

[19]E. Brooks Smith and Robert Meredith, eds., *Pilgrim Courage: From a Firsthand Account by William Bradford, Governor of Plymouth Colony: Selected Episodes from His Original History* Of Plimoth Plantation: *And Passages from the Journals of William Bradford and Edward Winslow* (Boston: Little, Brown and Company, 1962), 5-6.

now, most of you know who these people were. We will continue with their story next week.

June 13, 2010
John Robinson

Last week we talked about the village of Scrooby and the separatist congregation that formed there. We looked at William Brewster, and we traced his life up to the time of the congregation's move to the Netherlands—first to Amsterdam, and finally to the city of Leiden under Pastor John Robinson.

A little pamphlet called *The Mayflower Story*, put out by the Society of Mayflower Descendants, says that Leiden in 1608 was called "the most beautiful city in Europe." There was an important university in Leiden, and Pastor Robinson became a lecturer there. The Congregationalists from Scrooby began to put down roots. Even though they had been farmers, shopkeepers, and tradesmen of various kinds back in England, they went to work in the textile industry, learning the Dutch language, and their children attended the Dutch public schools.

According to *The Mayflower Story*, ". . . Pastor John Robinson, for loftiness of spirit and breadth of vision, has hardly a parallel. . . . He laid down the principle that the human conscience is of too subtle a nature to be circumscribed. . . . His people were intensely devoted to him."[20] The book *Saints and Strangers* tells us that Robinson was "a gentle, wise, and resourceful leader. He was very pleasant and courteous in manner. . . . He despised hypocrites. . . . [He] preached three times a week . . . to the great comfort and content of his disciples. . . . [He] had a level head in business affairs and other worldly matters. Quick to sense hidden dangers, he skillfully led his flock around many a pitfall. . . ."[21]

Robinson, for all his gentle ways, could speak harshly. In 1608, a bishop encouraged him to recognize the Church of England as his mother. Robinson answered, "So may she be, and yet not the Lord's wife." John Von Rohr reports that Robinson added a comment "that even a mother can have children by fornication!" In 1610, Robinson wrote *A Justification of Separation from the Church of England*. He wrote in that book that the

---

[20]Raymond F. Hughes, *The Mayflower Story* (Plymouth: General Society of Mayflower Descendants, 1973), 3.

[21]Willison, 84.

Church of England, "till it be separated and free from the world, and the prince of the world that reigneth in it, cannot possibly be the true church of God, the wife of Christ." However, he said, "A company, consisting though of but two or three, separated from the world, and gathered into the name of Christ by a covenant, is a church, and so has the whole power of Christ."[22] This is the Congregational concept of "the gathered church." Jesus said in Matthew 18:20, "For where two or three are gathered together in my Name, there am I in the midst of them."

By 1617, Robinson was feeling less hostile to the Anglican church. He and William Brewster drew up "The Seven Articles," expressing agreement with the Anglican Articles of Religion and calling for reconciliation with the Church of England. However, some "notes of explanation" were attached that undercut the conciliatory message: "Touching the ecclesiastical ministry . . . we do wholly and in all points agree with the French Reformed churches, according to their public confession of faith."[23]

Harry Butman calls the Seven Articles "a fruitless attempt to gain the favor of hostile King James I. . . . It never reached James, and its failure led to the decision of the Pilgrims to migrate to America."[24] Some histories claim that the Pilgrims came to the New World for religious freedom. But they had that already in Holland. Others say that they were concerned about their children becoming too Dutch and forgetting that they were English, and some point out the wide-open nature of Dutch society and its corrupting influence on the young.

But it was more than that. The theology of the people we have come to know as the Pilgrims taught that they were the new Chosen People and that England was the new Promised Land. When they were forced to leave England, they had to identify somewhere else as the Promised Land, and it would not be the Netherlands. The new Chosen People had to find a new Promised Land. Like Abraham, they would travel far to the west, into the unknown wilderness.[25]

---

[22]Von Rohr, 18.

[23]Walker, 90-91.

[24]Butman, *Symbols*, 6.

[25]Edward Johnson, *Wonder-Working Providence of Sions Saviour in New England* (Andover: Warren F. Draper, 1867), partially reprinted in *Readings in the*

June 20, 2010
William Bradford

Except for Miles Standish, John Alden, and Priscilla Mullins, the most famous of the Pilgrims was probably William Bradford. Bradford was born in Austerfield, Yorkshire, in March 1589. By age seven he was an orphan, but as a teenager he came under the influence of William Brewster, who would be a surrogate father to him. Bradford would later be the longest-serving governor of Plymouth Colony and also its best-known historian, but in 1608 when the Scrooby congregation moved to Holland, he was only nineteen years old. (His youth had served him well the year before, when the congregation had been betrayed by the Dutch skipper, because Bradford was released from custody immediately, while the others had to spend time in jail.) Five years after emigrating, having become a naturalized Dutch citizen, he was married to Dorothy May, another English separatist who was only sixteen years old, in Leiden. He was probably glad to be married and out of the Brewsters' house, because he had been living with them on a street called Stink Alley! Bradford was mostly self-taught, but he evidently did a good job of educating himself, because he could speak French, Dutch, and Latin. Many years later, when he was an old man in America, he would teach himself Hebrew so that he could read the Old Testament in the original language.[26]

Most historians treat Bradford very well, but George Willison, the author of *Saints and Strangers*, is a little less enthusiastic: "Bradford was disingenuous at times. He was not above politic distortion of facts, and did not hesitate to suppress whole chapters in the history of his brethren. . . . His remarks about those who opposed him or his brethren in any way are often unreliable and always savage. . . . But for all that, Bradford is always an informed and usually a safe guide. . . . One can scarcely write or speak a word about the Pilgrims without leaning heavily upon him. Every American conscious of his heritage, particularly of its democratic roots, is infinitely beholden to him."[27] Harry Butman is more admiring: "The Pilgrim band has

---

History and Polity of the National Association of Congregational Christian Churches, ed. Arlin T. Larson (Demorest: Piedmont College, 1997).

[26]Lindsey, 1-3.

[27]Willison, 4.

its own superlative chronicler in William Bradford, child of the Elizabethan age of noble expression."[28]

By 1620, only thirty-one years old, Bradford had become one of the recognized leaders of the congregation. That June, the little church observed "a day of humiliation."[29] Pastor Robinson preached on a text from I Samuel: "And David's men said unto him, 'See, we be afraid here in Judah: how much more if we come to Keilah against the host of the Philistines?' Then David asked counsel of the Lord again."

Bradford describes the congregation's debate before making the decision to go to the New World: "They discussed the advantages and disadvantages of going to one of those vast and unpeopled countries of America. Although these countries were fit and fruitful to live in, they had no civilized people, only savage brutish men who ranged up and down like wild beasts. . . . Those who desired to move to America argued that all great and honorable actions are always accompanied with great difficulties. . . . All of these difficulties . . . might through the help of God . . . be borne and overcome."[30]

In July 1620, the church had two ships, the *Mayflower* and the *Speedwell*. The first step of the voyage would be the passage across the English Channel on board the *Speedwell*. Historian Nathaniel Philbrick comments: "For Bradford and his wife, Dorothy, the parting . . . was particularly painful. They had decided to leave their three-year-old son, John, behind in Holland. . . . Whether he realized it or not, Bradford was inflicting his own childhood experience on his son: for a time, at least, John would be, for all intents and purposes, an orphan."[31]

Bradford's account of the departure from Holland would give the group the name by which we know them today: "So they left that goodly and pleasant city which had been their resting place twelve years; but they knew they were pilgrims. . . ."[32]

---

[28]Butman, *Lord's Free People*, 22.

[29]Willison, 119.

[30]Smith and Meredith, 15-16.

[31]Nathaniel Philbrick, *Mayflower: A Story of Courage, Community, and War* (New York: Viking, 2006), 23.

[32]Smith and Meredith, 19.

June 27, 2010
Edward Winslow

We have been in a biographical mode these past few weeks, looking at major leaders of the Scrooby-Leiden-Plymouth congregation. We have discussed William Brewster, John Robinson, and William Bradford. Before we move on to continue the story of that congregation, we will look at the fourth and youngest of the most important leaders of the group, Edward Winslow. (I suppose I could call him Uncle Ed, since his brother John was my ancestor a mere fourteen generations back.)

Edward Winslow was born in 1595 in Worcestershire. After serving his apprenticeship in London, where he met William Brewster, he became a printer. In 1617, he was traveling in the Netherlands. It is said that he was of somewhat higher birth than most of the others who would be called Pilgrims, and that he was on the "grand tour" of the Continent, traditionally made by young English gentlemen. In Holland he ran into some of the congregation from Scrooby, and he joined the church. He married Elizabeth Barker the following year in Leiden.

Winslow was among those who went to America on the *Mayflower* in 1620. (His friend William Brewster was also aboard, but apparently sailed under an assumed name to escape the English authorities.) Winslow would sign the Mayflower Compact, and his wife would be one of the many who died in the first hard winter. We will look at all those events later, but right now we are following the very interesting life of Edward Winslow.

George Willison says, "Winslow was suave and plausible—'a cunning, smooth-tongued fellow,' said one critic—possessed of a nice sense of tact and the good sense to use it, rare qualities among the Pilgrims."[33] This tact served him and the colony well in later years, and it would make him an important figure in Congregationalism far beyond New England. Esther Lindsey gives examples of what we today would call "people skills": in 1621, "while Governor Carver was negotiating the treaty with [Chief] Massasoit, Winslow served as . . . hostage on Strawberry Hill with the Wampanoag [Indian]s until Massasoit and his twenty braves returned. This was the beginning of a life-long friendship between Winslow and Massasoit, which was so influential in maintaining the peace treaty that lasted for forty years,

---

[33]Willison, 182.

until Massasoit died in 1661. On a trip that Winslow and Hopkins took with Squanto as guide, to discover the lay of the land and the number and character of the Indians, they arrived at Massasoit's headquarters. On affirming the peace treaty, Winslow presented Massasoit with a red horseman's coat trimmed with white lace. To show his appreciation, Massasoit offered the visitors, in the best Indian tradition, a night's bedding with himself, his wife, and two aides, all in the chief's bed. Later, Winslow wrote, 'We were worse weary of our lodging than of our journey.' "[34]

Winslow would become an important citizen of Plymouth Colony, with a large estate, a huge library by the standards of the time, and a fine home that was used as the first school and the first church meetinghouse until a schoolhouse and a church building could be built. He succeeded Miles Standish as the colony's military leader; he served as assistant governor once, and as governor three times. But Winslow was important to the colony, and to the history of Congregationalism, in England as well as in New England. Not only was he, like Bradford, one of the historians of the colony, what today we might call a public-relations expert, but he acted as the colony's ambassador to England for many years (as well as to various Indian tribes).

Congregationalism was significant in the history of England, as well as in that of America. Oliver Cromwell, a Congregationalist, became Lord Protector of Great Britain, replacing the king, after the Puritans won the English Civil War. Cromwell met Winslow and made him an official in his government, and after 1646, Edward Winslow never returned to America. In 1654, he became commissioner of a British fleet that was sent to take the West Indies from Spain, and he died at sea the following year.

---

[34]Lindsey, 5-7.

July 18, 2010
Preparing for the Voyage

It is unavoidable that things will be somewhat simplified in our history books. In our time, travel is pretty easy. You just board that train, that airplane, that bus, that ship—or you simply slip behind the wheel of your car—and you go. We could be tempted to think that when the Pilgrims finally decided to go to America, they just went. But it wasn't that simple.

For one thing, the people from Scrooby were fugitives from justice in their own country, and most of them were still subjects of King James. The British government could have made trouble for them, but providentially the king and his advisers could see that it was to their advantage to get these troublemakers completely out of Europe. If they were exiling themselves into the western wilderness, so much the better. So a royal patent was granted in February 1620. However, even though they were for the most part hardworking and thrifty people, the Pilgrims were not wealthy, so the journey had to be financed. An arrangement was made with some London businessmen who called themselves the Merchant Adventurers, in which any profits of the colony for the first seven years would be divided between the colonists and the Adventurers. Originally, the Pilgrims intended to settle in the northern parts of Virginia, and their patent had to be amended to cover the place where they actually did settle, near Cape Cod.

Even the above description is oversimplified, because the patent and the funding were finally obtained only after about three years of planning and negotiations and fierce debate among the congregation. Some wanted to emigrate to Jamestown or to other parts of Virginia, while others preferred a number of other destinations, including even Guiana. While the funding came from the Merchant Adventurers, the patent—royal permission to establish a colony—came through a group called the Virginia Company, which had all kinds of internal problems of its own, with the threat of bankruptcy hanging over its head, the resignation of a key officer, and a struggle over his replacement. In addition, the Adventurers wanted to protect their interests, so they insisted that some of their business associates who were not Congregationalists (and in some cases not even Christians) go along on the voyage to the New World. This caused concern among the Pilgrims, and historians commonly distinguish between the church people and those others, designating them the "saints" and the "strangers."

Some of the saints were upset with the agreement with the Adventurers, because it meant that even their houses and yards would be included in the division of assets between the colonists and the London merchants. Many people fussed at their agents—Deacon Robert Cushman, future Governor John Carver, and Thomas Weston—about several provisions in the contract, but the agents replied that this was the best bargain they were going to get, unless they wanted to stay in Holland indefinitely. Not only was there a struggle between the Pilgrims and their agents, so that Cushman at one point accused the others of defying God's will, "like Jonah [fleeing to] Tarshish,"[35] but the agents themselves were arguing among themselves. Another wrinkle was the fact that William Brewster was in London for some of the negotiations, and he and Winslow had been publishing some very incendiary tracts against the royal government and the Church of England, so he was wanted by the authorities and had to be kept hidden.

Finally, in June 1620, came the departure from Leiden, Pastor Robinson staying with those who remained in Holland, and promising the Pilgrims in a moving dockside sermon that there was "more truth and light yet to break forth from God's Holy Word."[36] That still was not the end of the difficulties. Brewster still had to remain hidden. There were two ships, but the *Speedwell* proved unseaworthy. There were still more delays, with more disagreements about business issues, and only some of the *Speedwell* passengers were able to fit on board the *Mayflower*. But at last, in September 1620, the *Mayflower* set sail from Plymouth, England, to what would later become Plymouth, Massachusetts.

---

[35]Willison, 117.

[36]Arthur Rouner, Jr., *The Congregational Way of Life* (Oak Creek: Congregational Press, 1972), 5.

August 1, 2010
Voyage of the Mayflower

We left off last week with the Pilgrims just beginning their voyage to the New World. It was a long voyage, taking two and a half months, and the seas were stormy. There were one hundred two passengers, only forty-one of them from the church at Leiden. The *Mayflower* was a cargo vessel, not a passenger ship, and the living quarters were very cramped. There was no privacy, no showers or bathtubs, nothing but a few chamber pots for toilets, and only very simple food. This was no luxury liner!

Some of the sailors were unfriendly toward their passengers. William Bradford, in his picturesque way, describes what happened to one of the crew: "And I may not omit here a special work of Providence. There was a proud and very profane young man, one of the seamen, of a lusty, able body, which made him the more haughty. He was always blaming the poor people for being sick and cursing them daily, and went so far as to tell them he hoped to help cast half of them overboard before they came to their journey's end and then to make merry with their goods. If anyone gently reproved him, he would swear most bitterly. But it pleased God before they came half-seas over, to smite this young man with a painful disease, of which he died in a desperate manner, and so was himself the first thrown overboard and buried at sea. Thus his curses lit on his own head, and it was an astonishment to all his fellows, for they noted it to be the just hand of God upon him."[37]

Of course, many people were seasick during the voyage. There were other, more serious illnesses, but only one passenger died, a young servant named William Butten. John Howland had a narrow escape when he fell overboard during a storm, but with some difficulty he was rescued. One child was born. Since he was born upon the ocean, he was given the first name of Oceanus. He was the son of Stephen Hopkins, ancestor of Norman Yassany of our church. Probably, it never would have occurred to James Chilton and Stephen Hopkins that two of their descendants, Norm and I, would be members of a Congregational church on the other side of the North American continent in the twenty-first century. (By the way, the Society of Mayflower Descendants once estimated that about half the citizens of the United States are descended from at least one *Mayflower* passenger, whether they know it or not.)

---

[37]Smith and Meredith, 23.

At one point, the ship was in serious danger of sinking. There was a main beam, holding the ship together amidships, and it cracked during a ferocious storm. What was described as an "iron jack screw"[38] was found, and with that the beam was raised so that a supporting post could be placed under it. This was not ordinary equipment for a seagoing vessel, and some historians believe that it was probably the iron screw that was part of Brewster and Winslow's printing press. If that is true, then the same press that had made Brewster a wanted man now saved all their lives.

Finally, in November 1620, the *Mayflower* anchored in New England. By the way, New England had been named by Captain John Smith, who had also already named Plymouth, even though there was not yet a settlement there. (John Smith had offered to be the Pilgrims' military leader, but Miles Standish was chosen instead.) Providentially, Plymouth was empty of people, for the local Indians had all died of a serious illness. The only survivor was Squanto, who along with Samoset was such a help to the Pilgrims in their early years.

Two passengers died while the ship was at anchor. Dorothy Bradford, wife of William, went overboard and drowned. Nobody to this day knows whether it was an accident or suicide. (Remember, William and Dorothy had left their little boy behind in Holland.) The other death was my ancestor James Chilton. Along with Stephen Hopkins and others, he had signed the Mayflower Compact, but he did not survive to set foot in New England. However, one tradition says that his daughter Mary was the first female passenger to put her foot on Plymouth Rock.

Next time, we will look at the Mayflower Compact and its importance.

---

[38]Kate Caffrey, *The Mayflower* (New York: Stein and Day, 1974), 109.

August 15, 2010
The Mayflower Compact

The Mayflower Compact is an extremely short, but at the same time an extremely important, document. Except for the forty-one signatures at the bottom, the following words are the whole thing: "In the Name of God, Amen. We whose names are underwritten, the loyal subjects of our dread sovereign lord, King James, by the grace of God, of Great Britain, France, and Ireland king, Defender of the Faith, etc. Having undertaken, for the glory of God, and advancement of the Christian faith and honor of our king and country, a voyage to plant the first colony in the northern parts of Virginia, do by these presents, solemnly and mutually, in the presence of God, and one of another, covenant and combine ourselves together into a civil body politic, for our better ordering and preservation and furtherance of the ends aforesaid; and by virtue hereof to enact, constitute, and frame such just and equal laws, ordinances, acts, constitutions, and offices, from time to time, as shall be thought most meet and convenient for the general good of the Colony: unto which we promise all due submission and obedience. In witness whereof we have hereunder subscribed our names at Cape Cod, the 11th of November, in the year of the reign of our sovereign lord King James; of England, France, and Ireland the eighteenth, and of Scotland the fifty-fourth. Anno Domini 1620."[39] That is the whole document.

Why was the document written, and why was it signed before the passengers disembarked? It seems that some of the "strangers" had been heard to say that they would go their own way once they got to America, and that they would not be subject to the leaders of the Leyden congregation. Those leaders discussed the problem, and they soon decided that their church covenant was not adequate, since not all the colonists were members of their church. They realized that they also needed a covenant to establish the civil government. It all followed logically from their immediate circumstances and from their custom of following a church covenant, but this was really a radical act.

Even today, Great Britain does not have a written constitution. English people speak of their "constitution," but what they really mean is a

---

[39]Paul M. Angle, ed., *By These Words: Great Documents of American Liberty, Selected and Placed in Their Contemporary Settings* (San Francisco: Rand McNally & Company, 1954), 3-4.

supposedly common understanding of how the government ought to behave, an understanding that comes from history and tradition and the development of common law on a case-by-case basis. But the idea of a written constitution, new and radical as it was, occurred naturally to the Pilgrims for at least two reasons: (1) As already noted, they were used to living under a written church covenant, and (2) They were used to living under the authority of the written Word of God. It is not a great logical leap from the idea that God could put His Law into written form to the concept of a written constitution that would be the supreme law, authorizing all lesser laws that might be made in "a civil body politic." (Notice, too, how the Compact provides for the *occasional* enactment of laws, *as they are needed for the common good*. Would this be an apt description of how Congress works today?)

These Pilgrims had come from a country still bound by a medieval class system. It would not be surprising if it had seemed normal to them to establish their own little aristocracy in which the "saints" would lord it over the "strangers," but the signatures on the document include both saints and strangers, both masters and servants, educated and uneducated, older and younger. The signatures were broadly representative of the population of the newborn colony.

Another important detail to notice is that the purpose of planting the colony and the purpose of establishing a civil government are both said to be the same: "for the glory of God and advancement of the Christian faith." This is a strong argument in favor of the idea that America was founded as a Christian nation and that Christian principles should govern the people. That idea was still alive in 1776, when the Declaration of Independence spoke of the God-given rights of individual human beings who got together and instituted governments in order to secure those rights.

August 22, 2010
Plymouth Colony

We will say just a few more things about Plymouth Colony before we go on to other aspects of Congregationalism. Of course, there was the first hard winter, in which half the colonists—about fifty people—died. Most of the nursing and cooking and general care of the sick and of the other survivors fell on the teenage girls, including my ancestor Mary Chilton. Without the good work of those girls, even more would have died.

The following year was the famous first Thanksgiving. Many schoolchildren in our day are taught that this was a celebration held to thank the Indians for their help. It is true that the Indians were present at the feast. Not only did they eat the food provided by the Pilgrims, but they also brought five deer with them. However, in the book called *Mourt's Relation*, written at Plymouth and published in London in 1622, the author says, "Although it be not always so plentiful as it was at this time with us, yet by the goodness of God, we are so far from want that we often wish you partakers of our plenty."[40] So the Pilgrims knew Who was the ultimate Source of their blessings. They gave thanks to God.

There were, unfortunately, occasional conflicts with the Indians—some of them deadly—during the history of Plymouth Colony. But the friendship between Bradford and Massasoit, the Wampanoag chief, developed into a peace treaty between the Wampanoag tribe and the Pilgrims that lasted until 1675, after both Massasoit and Bradford had died. Nevertheless, relations with non-white people were not entirely idyllic. My ancestor Mary Chilton married John Winslow, brother of Governor Winslow. When John died in 1674, in his will he left Mary a human being, whom he described as "my Negro girl Jane."[41]

However, some things that are sometimes laid at the feet of the Pilgrims are not really their fault. It is true that Salem was a satellite of Plymouth, and its church produced a marvelous one-sentence covenant in 1629: "We covenant with the Lord and one with another and do bind ourselves in the presence of God to walk together in all His ways, according as

---

[40]Willison, 196.

[41]Robert M. Sherman, ed., *Mayflower Families through Five Generations* (Plymouth: General Society of Mayflower Descendants, 1978), vol. 2, p. 8.

He is pleased to reveal Himself unto us in His blessed Word of truth."[42] But the Salem witch trials, sometimes blamed on the Pilgrims, occurred after the end of Plymouth Colony's independent existence. Plymouth had been absorbed into Massachusetts Bay Colony in 1691.

Then there is the famous story of the Pilgrims' so-called "experiment with communism," often recounted in somewhat anachronistic terms. A pamphlet put out during the Cold War by the Society of Mayflower Descendants claims, "The Pilgrims were firm in their belief in the free-enterprise system and that each should reap the rewards of his own labor. In the beginning, the colony was run on a communal basis. . . . It was the collectivists' dream."[43] And it was true that this system failed. There was a severe food shortage. Bradford says that it was decided "that they should set corn every man for his own and in that regard trust to themselves. And so [they] assigned to every family a parcel of land. . . . This had very good success, for it made all hands very industrious, so as much more corn was planted than otherwise would have been. The women now went willingly into the field, which before would allege weakness and inability, whom to have compelled would have been thought great tyranny and oppression."[44] But this was not really a voluntary "experiment with communism," as it is sometimes represented. The Pilgrims were practical people, and they had common sense and a good knowledge of human nature. The so-called experiment with communism was merely the result of their following the unsatisfactory provisions of their agreement with the Merchant Adventurers. They wisely abrogated the agreement when they saw that it was leading to disaster.

After all this time discussing the Pilgrims, it may surprise you when I say this: although they had a great influence on the founding of our republic, they were not in the mainstream of Congregationalism, and the Puritans would have greater influence. More on that next week!

---

[42]Butman, *Symbols*, 7.

[43]Hughes, 9.

[44]Caffrey, 182.

August 29, 2010
Massachusetts Bay Colony

In the beginning, the Puritan movement was very broad. In its mildest form, it was a group of Christians who wanted to remain within the established Church of England, but to have the freedom to use or not to use, as each congregation chose, the prescribed rituals, liturgy, prayer book, and priestly vestments of the state church. In its most extreme form, it was represented by the separatists—people like the Pilgrims of Plymouth Colony—who insisted that the local congregation was the whole Church, without ties to any higher earthly authority and without accountability to any other congregation. In the middle were those who would develop into the Presbyterians and Baptists. Also in the middle—but closer to the separatist side—was the group that became known as the Independents, and only later as Congregationalists. These were people like us, who believed in the integrity and sufficiency of the local congregation as a living instance of the Body of Christ, subject to no authority beyond its local leaders (except for the headship of Jesus Christ), but in fellowship with other churches.

In American history, the term "Puritan" is customarily used to describe the non-separatist Puritans who started their own colonies that were completely independent of Plymouth, in order to distinguish them from the Pilgrims. Almost as famous as the *Mayflower* was the *Arbella*, the ship that brought the founders of Massachusetts Bay Colony, along with their colonial charter and their first governor, John Winthrop, in 1630. It was Winthrop who gave his famous message aboard the *Arbella* in which he quoted Jesus' Sermon on the Mount and described the new colony as a shining city on a hill. In our recent history, we remember that Ronald Reagan particularly loved to quote that phrase from Winthrop's sermon, reminding us that America itself is supposed to be the gleaming city on a hill whose light would benefit the rest of the world.

John von Rohr, in his history of the Congregational movement, says, "Altogether some sixty ministers arrived in Massachusetts between the years 1630 and 1641, the vast majority of whom were of non-Separatist Congregational persuasion."[45] No wonder that the separatists who lived in the settlements of Plymouth Colony were swallowed up in a few decades by the Puritans of Massachusetts Bay Colony! Von Rohr reports that the new colony

---

[45]Von Rohr, 63.

had a form of representative government, but it did not believe that government received its just powers from the consent of the governed. It believed instead that government received its authority from God. There was some sense of the separate duties of church and state, although political leaders were expected to be godly men, and church leaders were expected to support the civil authority. However, it was required that there would be only one authorized church in a community, and that would be a Congregational church. In fact, the Congregational church would continue to be legally the established church in Massachusetts until well after the independence of the United States and the ratification of the Constitution and the Bill of Rights (including, of course, the First Amendment). In 1833, the state of Massachusetts finally enacted a law disestablishing the Congregational church as the official church of that state. (By the way, I suppose that means that antidisestablishmentarianism was not very popular in Massachusetts by then.)

Thomas Hooker, a New England pastor, published his Congregational Principles in 1645. Here are some of them: "Visible saints are the only true and meet matter whereof a visible church should be gathered. . . ." In other words, the true church consists only of true believers. "There is no [Presbyterian] church . . . in the New Testament. . . . Ordination is only a solemn installing of an officer into the office unto which he was . . . called. . . . Consociation of churches should be used, as occasion doth require. Such consociations and synods have allowance to counsel and admonish other churches, as the case may require. And if they grow obstinate in error, [the synod] should renounce the right hand of fellowship with them. But [synods] have no power to excommunicate."[46] This is not separatism, but true Congregationalism.

---

[46]Walker, 143-147.

September 12, 2010
Westminster and Cambridge

One important document of the Puritan Revolution, also known as the English Civil War, was the Westminster Confession, the result of a meeting of Puritan pastors in Westminster, England, that began in 1643. Probably the most famous part of the Confession, still quoted frequently today, is this, from an appendix to the Confession called the Westminster Shorter Catechism: "Man's chief end is to glorify God and to enjoy Him forever."[47] Amen! However, the Confession was basically a Presbyterian document. Congregationalists agreed with the theology of the Confession, except for its *ecclesiology*, its teachings about church government. So, beginning in 1646 in Cambridge, Massachusetts, a synod of New England Congregationalist pastors put out a revision of the Westminster Confession that came to be known as the Cambridge Platform, or as the Platform of Church Discipline.

Harry Butman describes the Platform as "a ponderous and thorny document." He also points out that, while the Platform answers the Westminster Confession very eloquently by clearly stating the Congregational principles of church government, at the same time the Platform violates those same principles. Remember that Congregationalism recognizes no authority above the local church except the authority of Jesus Christ. But the Cambridge Synod, which produced the Platform, was called by the Massachusetts legislature; and the Platform was declared to be, in Butman's words, "the legally recognized standard of Congregationalism."[48]

Of course, Dr. Butman is right. Still, the Platform has some very good things to say about what Congregationalism is. For one thing, the document maintains that the form of church government has not been left up to human decision (and, ironically, this of course would include the decisions of the Massachusetts legislature). These Puritan divines were firmly convinced that Congregational polity was God's plan for His Church: "The parts of church government are all of them exactly described in the Word of God, being parts or means of instituted worship according to the Second Commandment, and therefore to continue one and the same unto the appearing of our Lord Jesus

---

[47]Philip Schaff, ed., *The Creeds of Christendom* (Grand Rapids: Baker Book House, 1990), vol. 3, p. 676.

[48]Butman, *Symbols*, 8.

Christ, as a Kingdom that cannot be shaken, until He shall deliver it up unto God, even the Father. So that it is not left in the power of men, officers, churches, or any state in the world to add or diminish or alter anything in the least measure therein."[49]

What is the Church? The Platform tells us, giving us a definition of the catholic, or universal, Church, which includes all the saints in heaven and on earth. The definition includes the statement, "We deny a universal visible Church." In other words, no earthly organization has the right to call itself the one and only Church, as the Roman Catholic Church and the Eastern Orthodox Church do, and as the Church of England maintained that it was, at least within the borders of the king's sovereign authority. The Platform then proceeds to distinguish between believers in heaven, who are the Church Triumphant, and us believers on earth, who are the Church Militant. Finally, it describes a local church as a living part of the Church Militant.

"The catholic Church is the whole company of those that are elected, redeemed, and in time effectually called from the state of sin and death unto a state of grace and [unto] salvation in Jesus Christ. This Church is either triumphant, or militant: triumphant, the number of them who are glorified in heaven; militant, the number of them who are conflicting with their enemies upon earth. This Militant Church is to be considered as invisible and visible: invisible in respect of their relation wherein they stand to Christ, as a body unto the Head, being united unto Him by the Spirit of God and faith in their hearts; visible, in respect of the profession of their faith, in their persons, and in particular churches. . . . A Congregational church is by the institution of Christ a part of the Militant visible Church, consisting of a company of saints by calling, united into one body by a holy covenant for the public worship of God and the mutual edification one of another in the fellowship of the Lord Jesus."[50] More on the Platform next week.

---

[49]Walker, 203.

[50]Ibid., 204-205.

September 19, 2010
More on the Cambridge Platform

As promised, we have more on the Cambridge Platform. Since it was produced by a committee of Congregationalists, you may not be surprised to learn that even though the Platform was merely a slight revision of the Westminster Confession, it still took the synod of ministers *five years*—from 1643 to 1648—to complete their work.

The Platform maintains that the Congregational church is the one envisioned by Jesus: "Every church appointed and ordained by Christ had a ministry ordained and appointed for the same: and yet plain it is that there were no ordinary officers appointed by Christ for any other than Congregational churches. . . ."[51]

When we remember that most evangelical Protestants in the United States today are still Dispensationalists, even in the twenty-first century still following the nineteenth-century innovations of Francis Darby in England, it is interesting to see how far our Congregational pioneers were from Darby's insistence that Israel and the Church are never to be identified with each other: "The Covenant, as it was that which made the family of Abraham and children of Israel to be a church and people unto God, so it is that which now makes the several societies of Gentile believers to be churches in these days."[52] Did you see the casual assumption that readers would agree that Israel was the Old Testament church?

"All believers ought, as God giveth them opportunity thereunto, to endeavor to join themselves unto a particular church. . . ."[53] The Cambridge divines had no patience for the attitude we see so often in our time, an attitude that probably existed in their time as well, the attitude often expressed in this way: "I don't need to go to church to be a Christian. After all, I can worship God in the great outdoors, whether I am on the mountains or in the woods or at the seashore. That's where I feel closest to him, not in a church building."

"The supreme [power in the Church] is the Lord Jesus Christ. . . . The Lord Jesus out of His tender compassion hath appointed and ordained officers.

---

[51]Ibid., 207.

[52]Ibid., 208.

[53]Ibid., 209.

. . .Officers for the church are justly accounted no small parts, they being to continue to the end of the world . . . for the perfecting of all the saints. . . . When Paul was to take his last leave of the church of Ephesus, he committed the care of feeding the church to no other but unto the elders of that church. ... Of elders (who are also in Scripture called bishops), some attend chiefly to the ministry of the word, as the pastors and teachers. Others attend especially unto rule, who are therefore called ruling elders."[54] It is worth noticing that this pattern is followed in several large American churches today, where there is an executive minister and a preaching minister.

"The office of a deacon is instituted in the Church by the Lord Jesus. ... The office and work of the deacons is to receive the offerings of the church, gifts given to the church, and to keep the treasury of the church. . . The office therefore being limited unto the care of the temporal good things of the church, it extends not unto the . . . Word and sacraments and the like. The ordinance of the Apostle and practice of the Church commends the Lord's Day as a fit time for the contributions of the saints."[55]

"Officers are to be called by such churches whereunto they are to minister. . . . A church, being free, cannot be subject to any but by a free election; yet when such a people do choose any to be over them in the Lord, then do they become subject and most willingly submit to their ministry in the Lord, [that is, to those ministers] whom they have so chosen."[56]

The "government of the church is a mixed government. . . . In respect of Christ . . . it is a *monarchy*; in respect of the . . . brotherhood of the church ... it resembles a *democracy*; in respect of the [elders], it is an *aristocracy*."[57]

Since we are not separatists, the Platform reminds us, "Although churches be distinct . . . and equal, and therefore have not dominion one over another, yet all the churches ought to preserve church communion one with another. . . ."[58]

---

[54]Ibid., 209-211.

[55]Ibid., 213.

[56]Ibid., 214.

[57]Ibid., 217-218.

[58]Ibid., 229-230.

September 26, 2010
The Levellers

To continue our story of the development of Congregationalism, we have to leave New England for the time being and return to England. A fact not often remarked on by historians is that by 1485, after a thousand years, the native Britons had finally had a sort of revenge on the Anglo-Saxon invaders. It took three or four centuries after the invasion of the Angles, Saxons, and Jutes in the fifth century before the German tribes became completely dominant and the nation became thought of as England, land of the Angles. The native British race either became a quiet underclass or retreated to Wales or Scotland or Ireland or Cornwall. Eventually the Anglo-Saxon kings themselves were displaced by Norsemen and Normans, and finally there was a new synthesis wherein the French-speaking Norman invaders became naturalized and English language and culture changed to accommodate what became the new England and the new Englishmen. But with Henry VII, the Tudors, who were Welsh, became the royal family. After Elizabeth I's death, the Stewarts, who were Scots, were the new royal family. However, this re-establishment of native British families at the head of the country was soon overshadowed by what was now a more important issue: the clash between parliamentary democracy and royal authority, which at the same time was a conflict between the Puritans and the Church of England.

Many historians write that there was more than one English Civil War, while others see all the conflicts as part of the same war. The conflicts lasted from 1642 to 1651. In the end King Charles I was executed, the parliamentary forces had won, Oliver Cromwell would soon become Lord Protector of England, and the Church of England was disestablished. England was officially a *commonwealth*, which is really the English equivalent of the more familiar Latin word *republic*. The Puritans had won, and they would remain dominant in England until the Restoration under Charles II in 1660. In the beginning, the Presbyterians were the strongest part of the Puritan movement, with the Baptists a small minority and the Congregationalists (who were also called Independents) gaining power until they finally became the most powerful group. Cromwell himself was an Independent, or a Congregationalist.

Important in the development of both Congregationalism and democratic government in England and America were the propagandists of the Puritan Revolution, notably the "Levellers," who were called that by their enemies, who thought that they were some kind of primitive Communists who wanted to bring all the people to the same social and economic level. They were really Puritans and what we today might call libertarians, who wanted to bring down the power of the king and of the Church of England and who also wanted equality among the Puritan factions. John Locke was a teenager at the time of the Levellers' writings. Locke, as you know, was the philosopher who is often said to have been the most influential on the Founding Fathers of the United States. But Locke's ideas did not suddenly write themselves on the blank slate of his mind. Many of those ideas came straight from the Levellers of the 1640's.

One of the Levellers' broadsides was *A Remonstrance of Many Thousand Citizens* in 1646, addressed to Parliament to protest infighting in the Puritan movement. This was written by a Baptist printer named Richard Overton. Some of what Overton says about the king sounds very much like what Jefferson would write more than a hundred years later in our Declaration of Independence: "The continual oppressors of the nation have been kings." This king has acted in that tradition by "his under-working with Ireland, his endeavor to enforce the parliament by the army raised against Scotland, his purpose of raising war . . . persisting in the most bloody war that ever this nation knew, to the wasting and destruction of multitudes of honest and religious people. Ye have experience that none but a king could do so great intolerable mischiefs, the very name of *King* proving a sufficient charm to delude many of our brethren in Wales, Ireland, England, and Scotland, too, so far as to fight against their own liberties. . . ."[59] More next week!

---

[59]Don M. Wolfe, ed., *Leveller Manifestoes of the Puritan Revolution* (New York: Humanities Press, 1967), 115.

October 3, 2010
Leveller Manifestoes

We continue this week with a few excerpts from the Leveller manifestoes of the English Civil War. These are of interest because they are usually directed against the Congregationalists, or Independents, who had become dominant in the Puritan government, although in many cases they are exactly in agreement with Congregational principles as we have come to understand them, and also with Constitutional principles as Americans have come to understand them.

"The Petition of March 1647" addresses the House of Commons, beginning with praise and ending with a series of demands for change. The writers say, "It is most thankfully acknowledged that ye have . . . suppressed the High Commission, Star Chamber, and Council Table, called home the banished, delivered such as were imprisoned for matters of conscience, and brought some delinquents to deserved punishment. That ye have suppressed the bishops and Popish lords. . . ."[60] After the praise comes language foreshadowing our Bill of Rights and our current views on religious tolerance: "That ye will take off all sentences, fines and imprisonments imposed on commoners . . . without due course of law or judgment of their equals. . . . That ye will permit no authority whatsoever to compel any person or persons to answer to questions against themselves. . . . That all statutes, oaths and covenants may be repealed so far as they tend, or may be construed, to the molestation and ensnaring of religious, peaceable, well-affected people for non-conformity or different opinion or practice in religion. That no man for preaching or publishing his opinion in religion in a peaceable way may be punished or persecuted as heretical by judges that are not infallible, but may be mistaken (as well as other men) in their judgments. . . ."[61]

In November 1647 "An Agreement of the People" was published by several regiments of the army, petitioning Parliament to adopt certain measures that we today take for granted, and again in part sounding very much like our Bill of Rights: "That the power of this [Parliament] and all future representatives of this nation is inferior only to theirs who choose them, and doth extend . . . to the enacting, altering, and repealing of laws; to the erecting

---

[60]Ibid., 135-136.

[61]Ibid., 139.

and abolishing of offices and courts . . . and generally to whatsoever is not expressly or impliedly reserved by the represented to themselves. That matters of religion and the ways of God's worship are not at all entrusted by us to any human power. . . ."[62]

The demand for religious freedom, not just for Congregationalists but for everyone, is also heard in "The Petition of September 11, 1648": "That you would not have followed the example of former tyrannous and superstitious Parliaments in making orders, ordinances or laws, or in appointing punishments concerning opinions [about] things supernatural, styling some blasphemies, others heresies, when . . . you know yourselves easily mistaken and [you know] that divine truths need no human helps to support them. . . ."[63]

In December of that year came an even more radical demand from the Levellers, in a pamphlet with the title "No Papist nor Presbyterian, but the Modest Desires and Proposals of Some Well-affected and Freeborn People": this was the demand that Parliament extend religious freedom *even to Roman Catholics*! This would have been too far-reaching even for the honest citizens of Plymouth Colony. "Some perhaps may here object that to grant thus much would be too much in favor of the Papists, whereunto we answer that . . . we bear them no more love than what one Christian is bound to show unto another, and . . . it cannot . . . be warranted by Scripture that they or any others that wear the title of Christians should be excluded. . . . And . . . we cannot say that they are . . . idolaters, as those mentioned in the Old Testament, who absolutely adored . . . the images of false gods, which these Papists (for ought we can learn) do not do, but do adore the image of the true God, and therefore cannot properly be called idolaters, at least in [the Scriptural] sense, but rather superstitious and Popish persons."[64]

---

[62]Ibid., 227.

[63]Ibid., 289.

[64]Ibid., 308-309.

October 10, 2010
Richard Overton

In the April 1990 issue of a journal called *The St. Croix Review* appeared an article titled "Richard Overton, Prophet of Freedom." I have the author's permission to quote extensively from his article. We mentioned Overton earlier as a leader in the Leveller movement, one of the factions in the English Civil War that, as we remarked last week, upheld key principles of Congregationalism as we know it, and of Constitutional government, even though it opposed the Congregational establishment under Oliver Cromwell.

According to that article, "The Levellers, whose strength was among the common soldiers and among what historians have described as the urban lower middle class [had] their greatest influence from 1645 through 1649. . . . Distinctive Leveller positions included demands for a written constitution, fuller suffrage, religious toleration for all groups including Catholics, the absence of any established church, freedom of speech and the press, an end to imprisonment for debt, the use of the English language in all legal proceedings. [Ever since the Norman Conquest, the language of the law had been French.] Since government's legitimate powers were given to it by the people, some Levellers held that English government had been illegitimate since 1066, when it was imposed by the Norman Conquest. . . . Historians agree that the Levellers were tragically ahead of their time. Probably the main reason that the Leveller movement lasted as long as it did was that it was useful to Cromwell [in playing the various factions of the Puritan movement against each other]. After executing King Charles in January 1649, Cromwell moved swiftly to bring Parliament to heel and to crush the Leveller movement.

". . . Charles Beard has highlighted the remarkable similarity between the opening sentences of the Declaration of Independence and several quotations from Leveller tracts, including [this one] from Overton. . . . 'By natural birth, all men are equally and alike born to like property, liberty, and freedom. . . .'

"Article I of our Bill of Rights is like these articles of Overton's: 'That all statutes made for the compulsion of persons to hear the Common Prayer Book and for the exercise of other Popish rites and ceremonies may be . . . taken away. . . . That strong provisions be made that [no one in authority] may in any wise [keep] any person or persons from . . . presenting any petition or petitions concerning their grievances [or] liberties to the High Court of Parliament.'

"These articles evoke our Fifth Amendment: 'That no free commoner of England be [forced] to answer to any interrogatories concerning himself in any criminal case. . . . That neither the High Court of Parliament nor any subordinate court . . . before . . . verdict of twelve men or other due process of law may take away any free commoner's life, liberty, goods, or freehold. . . .'

"This prohibition against cruel and unusual punishment sounds like Article VIII of our Bill of Rights: 'That according to the Law of God and the old law of the land, matters of theft may not be punished with death. . . .' "[65]

And to those who claim that John Locke was the philosopher behind the thinking of Jefferson and others of our Founders, listen to what Richard Overton said in 1646: "To every individual in nature is given an individual property by nature, not to be invaded or usurped by any: for everyone as he is himself, so he hath a self property, else could he not be himself, and on this no second may presume to deprive any of without manifest violation [of] the very principles of nature, and of the rules of equity and justice between man and man. . . ."[66]

In 1690, John Locke would write similar words: "Though the earth and all inferior creatures be common to all men, yet every man has a property in his own person."[67] It seems that the principles of our Declaration of Independence and Bill of Rights derive not so much from John Locke as from the thinking of those rebel Congregationalists of the Puritan Revolution.

---

[65]Robert Hellam, "Richard Overton, Prophet of Freedom," *The St. Croix Review* 23, no. 2 (April 1990): 56-59.

[66]Ibid., 60.

[67]Ibid.

October 17, 2010
The Savoy Declaration

A few weeks ago, we were looking at the Cambridge Platform, which was a Congregationalist revision of the Westminster Confession, drawn up by New England pastors. Ten years later, the Congregationalists in England did a similar thing. Feeling that the Westminster Confession, while sound in its general theology, was too Presbyterian, these English Congregationalists produced the Savoy Declaration in 1658. Perhaps sensing that the Puritan republic was almost at an end and that restoration of the monarchy was near, the preface to the document is very peaceful in tone, even declaring that Congregationalists were in agreement with every one of the thirty-nine Articles of Religion of the Church of England. The English Congregational pastors were more frugal with their time than their New England brethren were: while the Cambridge Platform took five years from start to finish, the Savoy Declaration took only eleven days! As the preface itself says, "It is therefore to be looked at as a great and special work of the Holy Ghost, that so numerous a company of ministers and other principal brethren should so readily, speedily, and jointly give up themselves unto such a whole body of truths that are after godliness."

Acknowledging that Congregationalism started out as Separatism, the preface goes on: "We confess that from the first every one . . . of our churches have been in a manner like so many ships . . . launched singly and sailing apart and alone in the vast ocean of these [tumultuous] times, [but] God ordered it for His high and greater glory . . . that all should be found to have steered their course by the same chart and to have been bound for one and the same port, and . . . the same holy and blessed truths . . . which are current . . . amongst all the other churches of Christ in the world should be found to be our [cargo]."[68]

The preface continues by saying that the principal differences between the Westminster Confession and the Savoy Declaration consist in what was left out of the latter: all provisions that supported a Presbyterian view of church polity, for example, and those statements that advanced a Presbyterian view of the relationship between church and state. Continuing, the preface says, "What we have laid down and asserted about churches and their government, we humbly conceive to be the order which Christ Himself hath appointed to be observed. . . . We are able to trace the footsteps of an

---

[68]Walker, 359.

independent Congregational Way in the ancientest customs of the churches, as also in the writings of our soundest Protestant divines, and [we are satisfied that we are in] full concurrence throughout, in all the substantial parts of church government, with our reverend brethren the old Puritan non-conformists, who being instant in prayer and much sufferings, prevailed with the Lord, and we reap with joy what they sowed in tears."[69]

One part of the Savoy Declaration that is an addition to the Westminster Confession is chapter 20, "Of the Gospel and of the Extent of the Grace Thereof." This may be regarded as an early creed of Congregationalism (but it was not the first creed to be drawn up by Congregationalists, even though we often allege that we are a "non-credal church"). We will finish by quoting a few key points from this chapter.

"The covenant of works being broken by sin . . . God was pleased to give unto the elect the promise of Christ, the Seed of the woman, as the means of calling them and begetting in them faith and repentance. [Thus] the Gospel . . . was revealed, and was . . . effectual for the conversion and salvation of sinners. This promise of Christ . . . is revealed only in and by the Word of God. . . . The revelation of the Gospel unto sinners . . . is merely of the sovereign will and good pleasure of God, not . . . by . . . any . . . improvement of men's natural abilities. . . . Although the Gospel be the only outward means of revealing Christ and saving grace, and is as such abundantly sufficient thereunto; yet that men . . . may be born again, there is moreover necessary an effectual, irresistible work of the Holy Ghost upon the whole soul. . . ."[70]

---

[69]Ibid., 364, 366.

[70]Ibid., 387-388.

October 24, 2010
Native Americans

We said earlier that relations with the American Indians were peaceful as long as John Winslow and Chief Massasoit of the Wampanoag tribe lived. After both men had died, a new ruler arose among the Wampanoags, named King Philip, and the terrible bloody conflict called King Philip's War started in the 1670's. But until then, peace and friendly relations prevailed.

Concern for the salvation of the Indians was present from the very beginning among the Congregationalists of New England. Massachusetts Bay Colony had an official seal with the picture of an American Indian calling out, "Come over and help us." This slogan is from Acts 16:9, Paul's vision of the man of Macedonia that led to the Christian Church's spread from Asia to Europe. Now it seemed to these modern Christians that the Church was being called to spread from Europe to America by evangelizing the Native Americans.

Congregational historian John von Rohr writes that this was considered so important that as early as the early 1640's the Massachusetts General Court tried "to organize missionary activity among the American Indian groups."[71] But it would be individuals, Von Rohr reports, who would take up the task. Thomas Mayhew, one of the founders of the settlement at Martha's Vineyard, would travel to the various islands along the Massachusetts coast to preach in the Indian villages, and he won many of them to the Christian faith. His first convert, Hiacoomes, became an ordained Congregational minister and was able to preach to his people in their own language. By the 1660's, there were two Congregational meetinghouses, serving Indians and led by Indians, and there were several more congregations without their own buildings. By this time there were ten American Indian preachers to serve these various congregations. Other members of the Mayhew family continued this mission for several decades.

In his history of the Christian Church, Justo González says that John Eliot had an even greater impact among American Indians than the Mayhew family had. Eliot was pastor of the Congregational church in Roxbury, Massachusetts. He became convinced that the Indians were the ten lost tribes of Israel, and González reports that Eliot began his work "among the Mohicans in 1646." González goes on to say that Eliot "gathered his converts

---

[71]Von Rohr, 109.

in villages that were ruled according to the law of Moses. There he taught them European agricultural methods and mechanical arts, so that they could sustain themselves. Great stress was also laid on the reading and study of the Bible, which Eliot translated into Mohican."[72] Eliot invented an alphabet for the Indian language, and he founded fourteen towns, composed of—and led by—what came to be called "Praying Indians." Many more were founded after Eliot's time.

Eliot's translation is said by most historians to have been written in Algonquian, not in Mohican, but the names of Indian tribes and languages are given differently by different writers. All agree that Eliot's American Indian Bible was the first to be published in America, before any Bible in the English language or in any other European tongue. Eliot's mission became so famous and so inspiring that, as historian Sydney Ahlstrom tells us, "Eliot and his colleagues . . . contributed to the interest that led Parliament in 1649 to incorporate the Society for the Propagation of the Gospel in New England—an organization that was still able to support Jonathan Edwards in his work among the Indians over a century later."[73]

Other publications in the native language besides the Bible included a catechism, translations of many Puritan tracts, and even the Cambridge Platform. The Praying Indian villages were organized around the Congregational church in each town, and they were governed in the same way as the English-speaking Puritan towns. John von Rohr tells us that "in the mid-1650s a building was constructed at Harvard to accommodate American Indian students, President Henry Dunster expressing the wish 'to make Harvard the American Indian Oxford as well as the New-English Cambridge.'"[74]

----

[72]Justo González, *The Story of Christianity* (San Francisco: HarperSanFrancisco, 1985), vol. 2, pp. 223-224.

[73]Sydney E. Ahlstrom, *A Religious History of the American People* (New Haven: Yale University Press, 1972), 157.

[74]Von Rohr, 111.

November 7, 2010
The Half-Way Covenant and Stoddardeanism

In his history of Congregationalism, John von Rohr explains, "From the very outset the English Separatist and non-Separatist proponents of a congregational polity, in opposition to the inclusive admission policies of a national church, insisted that church membership be limited to those who were personally qualified. Each local church must be a church of believers. Ideally this meant that . . . congregations were composed solely of true 'saints.' "[75] Remember that one of the Congregationalists' objections to the Church of England was that everyone within the parish boundaries of a local church was automatically considered to be a member of that church, so that congregations were likely to be a mixed group of Christians and non-Christians. Theologians in our tradition have insisted that the true Church is composed only of genuine believers, and that a local church ought to reflect that reality as much as possible, nobody being admitted into membership who could not give a clear testimony of having been born again.

Harry Butman comments, "The first generation [of Congregationalists in America] usually had [such a testimony], and since the children of the father were considered within the covenant, [a] problem did not arise until the third generation. By that time, there was a large number of people of good character, who were sound in doctrine and regular in attendance, but who lacked a personal religious experience. Could their children be baptized? . . . About this point of infant baptism a time of controversy arose which for complexity, intensity, number of meetings, and volume of bibliography, puts the Cambridge Platform debate to shame. [The controversy] lasted for 156 years from its inception in Dorchester to its final phase in Charlestown in 1780."[76]

In 1657, already twenty-three years after the issue first arose, the Massachusetts General Court called a group of Congregational pastors to an assembly. In 1662, that assembly decided to seek an agreement from a synod of all churches in Massachusetts. What came out of that synod would be called the Half-Way Covenant. Congregational churches had inherited the practice of infant baptism from their Calvinist forebears, and the children of

---

[75]Von Rohr, 94.

[76]Butman, *Symbols*, 9-10.

genuine believers were considered to be eligible for baptism. However, when those children grew up, even though they might not be able to testify to genuine faith, many of them still wanted their own children to be baptized. The Half-Way Covenant said that as long as such parents were not living openly sinful lives, and as long as they would say that they agreed with Congregational doctrine and with the covenant of their church, then their children could be baptized.

Seven years later, Solomon Stoddard became pastor of the church in Northampton. He noted the difficulty of keeping separate records of those who appeared to have a genuine faith and those who were merely eligible for baptism, and he decided that any persons who wanted to be baptized or who wanted their children to be baptized should not be denied unless they were living indecent lives. Holy Communion was also an issue, since up till then only true believers had been deemed eligible to take Communion. Stoddard opened that up to all people who were not living in open sin, whether or not those people laid any claim at all to being Christians. Of course, the problem now was that the Congregational churches had become very much like the Church of England that they had rebelled against a century earlier. Virtually anyone who lived near a church building could be considered a member of that church, be baptized, and receive the Lord's Supper, whether or not that person was a Christian. This view came to be known as Stoddardeanism, named after Solomon Stoddard.

It is somewhat ironic that Stoddard's much more famous grandson, Jonathan Edwards, would be dismissed in 1750 after twenty-four years as pastor of the Northampton church—even though he was a great preacher and a great philosopher and a hero of the revival called the Great Awakening—because, among other things, he was an opponent of Stoddardeanism.

November 14, 2010
Developments in Seventeenth-century Congregationalism

Congregational churches in the seventeenth century, according to John von Rohr, began to lose a few of their distinctive features. The role of the clergy was becoming more important, and the former refusal to draw a strict line between laity and clergy was softening. In the early years of the century, it was common in the New England churches for members to ask questions of the preacher after his sermon. That practice was condemned in the synod of 1637. The Cambridge Platform prohibited lay speaking in church without the permission of an elder. In most of the churches the old distinction between ruling elder and preaching elder was disappearing, in favor of each church having just one single pastor. Lay participation in ordination declined, as churches increasingly called upon ordained ministers from other churches to lay on hands in ordaining new pastors, and church councils in search of a new pastor or in conflict with a serving pastor were beginning to ask for help from outside clergy rather than resolve their issues in-house in a meeting of the membership.

Separatism was by now a thing of the past, with local churches joining together in what we now call associations. In those days, such groups were more likely to be called synods. Since there was still no clear separation of church and state, sometimes synods could be called by the colonial government or by the local magistrates. But more often such meetings were called by local churches in association. If it was felt that a particular congregation was not really walking in the Congregational Way, in an extreme case the synod could excommunicate a local church from fellowship in the association.

In the typical New England town, everyone was required to work six days a week. Idleness was not tolerated. However, everyone was just as firmly required *not* to work on Sunday, which was usually known not as Sunday, but as "the Sabbath." The meetinghouse was plain, with benches for the people, a high pulpit for the preacher, and a Communion table. There was no cross, and there were no other decorations. The preacher wore a black academic gown to demonstrate that he was a college or university graduate, along with the tabbed collar typical of Calvinist ministers. He wore no stole. A psalm was sung, usually out of the Bay Psalm Book that had been published in 1640. Sometimes there were many psalms set to music, and some of them had dozens of verses. There was no other music, and there were apparently no musical instruments. Prayer time lasted a long time, the congregation being allowed to lift up their requests out loud to the Lord. Sermons lasted at least an hour. The service would begin in the morning (and Communion would be in the morning once a month), and it would end in the afternoon (finishing with baptism as needed). The entire service could take three hours.

As noted last week, the sacrament of baptism was becoming controversial, with some Congregationalists questioning the practice of infant baptism, many stoutly defending it, and others struggling to find some kind of Scriptural guidance on the issue that could bring unity. But the sacrament of Communion was open to all true Christians—as long as they could testify that they were members of a Congregational church. Although there were Anglicans in the New England colonies, they were not allowed to take Communion in the Congregational churches. One historian explains that the Puritans justified limiting Communion in this way by calling it "a meal for the holy rather than a meal to produce holiness."[77]

Nevertheless, the view of many Congregational leaders was very broad. England had been chosen by God, they thought, to be the liberating agent that would free the whole Church from medieval corruption and superstition. But when England rejected the Congregational movement, God rejected England. New England would become what England should have been, and it would be a light to the nations, showing all the earth what a truly Christian republic could be and should be. Under the rule of Jesus Christ, their liberty would enlighten the world.

---

[77]Von Rohr, 106.

November 21, 2010
Harvard and Yale

As Pastor Joe said last week, the Congregational Church has historically valued an educated clergy. To that end, many colleges, universities, and seminaries have been founded by Congregationalists over the years. The first of these was Harvard College, now Harvard University, founded in Massachusetts in 1636. Harvard was named after John Harvard, a Congregational minister who had graduated from Cambridge University in England. When he died, John Harvard left his property and his library to the school. A book called *New England's First Fruits*, published a few years after Harvard's founding, explained why the institution was needed: "After God had carried us safe to New England, and we had builded our houses, provided necessaries for our livelihood, reared convenient places for God's worship, and settled the civil government, one of the next things we longed for and looked after was to advance learning and perpetuate it to posterity, dreading to leave an illiterate ministry to the churches when our present ministers shall lie in the dust."[78] John von Rohr summarizes the early curriculum at Harvard: "Hebrew, Aramaic, Greek, and Latin were learned; Scripture was read in the ancient tongues; logic and rhetoric were pursued; William Ames's *Marrow of Sacred Divinity* was memorized for catechetical recitation of basic Christian doctrine; and to bring together biblical knowledge and homiletical usage, the college president provided weekly declamations enabling students to learn how to combine logic and Scripture in refuting heresies and presenting truth. Likewise the spiritual development of ministerial students was encouraged through emphasis on worship and prayer. . . . As early as 1660 among the 135 ministerial leaders of the second generation, 116 were Harvard graduates."[79]

In 1701 in Connecticut, Yale College (now Yale University) was founded. Originally, every one of its trustees was a Congregational minister. Historian Sydney Ahlstrom says that "for a century and a half [Connecticut was] a stronghold of orthodox Puritanism, with Yale College as its intellectual center."[80] While Harvard had been founded specifically for the training of

---

[78]Ahlstrom, 149.

[79]Von Rohr, 172-173.

[80]Ahlstrom, 163.

Congregational ministers, Yale promised to train students for "employment both in Church and in civil state." Ahlstrom says that Yale was "committed to conserving the Puritan heritage; to this end its founding fathers donated to the nascent seminary of learning forty ponderous tomes [by various Calvinist] theologians. The regulations of the institution prescribed the Westminster Catechism and William Ames's *Marrow of Sacred Theology* as guides to scriptural truth. Divinity was to be taught and defended by the sixteenth-century logical methods of Petrus Ramus."[81] Among the great men who would graduate from Yale was Jonathan Edwards.

Many people have remarked, so it does not have to be dwelt on extensively here, that these colonial schools—as well as other Ivy League institutions that were founded by other denominations—started out to be explicitly Christian but over the years have grown increasingly hostile to Christianity. This has been true even of those schools that were founded as Christian seminaries, schools that might still say that they are teaching what they call Christianity but that advocate views that would be considered heretical by most of us who take the Bible seriously.

Other schools that were either founded as Congregational institutions or founded by Congregationalists or acquired by Congregationalists include Middlebury College in Connecticut in 1800, Hartford Seminary in Connecticut in 1833, Olivet College in Michigan in 1836, Pacific School of Religion in California in 1866, and Piedmont College in Georgia in 1897. Even Hartford Seminary and Pacific School of Religion are today very hospitable to non-Christian religions or to atheist and agnostic thought. However, I am glad to report that two of these schools are still in relationship with Congregationalism: one is Olivet College, home of the Congregational Foundation for Theological Studies; the other is Piedmont College, now affiliated with two denominations: the United Church of Christ and our own National Association of Congregational Christian Churches.

---

[81]Ibid., 295.

December 12, 2010
God's Controversy with New England

A few weeks ago, we mentioned King Philip's War. That began in 1675, when among the Wampanoag Indians there arose a king who knew not Bradford. The slaughter was terrible on both sides as the war dragged on for more than a year with horrific losses of life and property. Soon there was more chaos. Big fires destroyed large parts of Boston in 1676 and 1679. There was a very deadly smallpox epidemic. Several shipwrecks brought financial disaster to New England. And the Puritan republic in England was dead, with the Stuart monarchs restored to the throne and trying to force New England back into the Church of England.

Believing strongly in God's sovereignty, Congregationalist preachers thought that all this was the working out of God's judgment. Michael Wigglesworth called it "God's controversy with New England."[82] Increase Mather and others called a synod of Massachusetts churches in 1679. The synod issued a report called "The Necessity of Reformation," identifying the problem as unfaithfulness among the people—a loss of spiritual commitment, growing pride, lukewarm worship, unloving behavior, worldliness, and general rebellion against God. The delegates said that the Lord had "written His displeasure in dismal characters against us,"[83] evidently a reference to the handwriting on the wall in the book of Daniel. The answer, said the synod, was a renewal of the people's covenant relationship with God, and just as Josiah and Ezra in the Old Testament called for such a renewal, so did the New England pastors.

Each church was to have a periodic service in which the congregation formally renewed its commitment to the church covenant. As Arthur Rouner puts it, "Since the earliest days of Congregationalism this covenant has actually been a written document, an agreement among the original members of a church and between themselves collectively and Christ, that they would walk together as Christian brothers"[84] and sisters. Obviously, if the covenant was drawn up by the original members, then it is necessary for the later

---

[82]Von Rohr, 126.

[83]Walker, 426-427.

[84]Rouner, *Congregational Way*, 46-47.

members also to "own" the covenant in their time, so that it always remains the covenant of the living church.

Beyond that, the synod also published a Confession of Faith in 1680, which Sydney Ahlstrom calls "the first to be formally published in New England."[85] The Confession was based on the Savoy Declaration of the English Congregationalists, but there were important editorial changes, mostly to emphasize the concept of the covenant. Here are some of the passages of the document that were unique to New England, and not just quotations from the Savoy Declaration: "The supreme judge by which all controversies of religion are to be decided . . . can be no other than the holy Scripture delivered by the Spirit; into which Scripture so delivered, our faith is finally resolved."[86] The "doctrine of the Trinity is the foundation of all our communion with God and comfortable dependence upon Him."[87] "God . . . made a covenant of works and life . . . with our first parents and all their posterity in them, [but they] did willfully transgress the law of their creation and [did] break the covenant in eating the forbidden fruit."[88] ". . . The Lord was pleased to make a second [covenant], commonly called the Covenant of Grace. . . . Although this covenant hath been differently and variously administered . . . in the time of the Law, and since the coming of Christ in the flesh; yet . . . it is one and the same; upon the account of which various dispensations, it is called the Old and New Testament."[89] "It pleased God . . . to choose and ordain the Lord Jesus, His only begotten Son, according to a covenant made between them both, to be the Mediator between God and man. . . . [He] underwent the punishment due to us, which we should have borne and suffered. . ."[90] "As repentance is to be continued through the whole course of our lives . . . it is every[one's] duty to repent of his particular known sins. . . . Such is the provision which God hath made through Christ in the Covenant of Grace for

---

[85]Ahlstrom, 160.

[86]Walker, 369.

[87]Ibid., 370.

[88]Ibid., 373-374.

[89]Ibid., 375.

[90]Ibid., 375-376.

the preservation of believers unto salvation. . . ."[91] Old Testament ceremonies were "the legal administration of the Covenant of Grace,"[92] from which New Testament believers are free.

[91]Ibid., 382.

[92]Ibid., 389.

December 19, 2010
Witch Hunts

To be perfectly honest, I have wanted to ignore this topic, since it reflects badly on early New England Congregationalism. But my conscience says we need to look at it.

According to Peter Marshall, Jr., in the late 1600's many women who called themselves "witches" actually hung out shingles and advertised their services in the New England towns. Most people did not give them more credence than most of us give fortune tellers. But in 1692 in Salem, Massachusetts, several teenage girls experienced convulsions, and they decided that some of the town's citizens were in league with Satan and had caused these symptoms. The accusations of the girls, and later of others, were deemed to be "spectral evidence" and were taken seriously by the courts. There were trials, and there were convictions.

This hysteria lasted for five months. During that time, twenty people—fourteen women and six men—were hanged after having been convicted of witchcraft. Others died in prison. In those times, of course, pressure was routinely applied against prisoners, and sometimes they were tortured, so there were confessions. There were accusations against others, also, something like what we call "turning state's evidence" today, from prisoners trying to save their own skins.[93]

Puritan preachers like Cotton Mather are often accused of having encouraged these witch hunts. But John von Rohr maintains that in fact, Cotton Mather and his father, Increase Mather, were voices of restraint. The Mathers said that "spectral evidence" was not strong enough for conviction in a court of law.[94] Soon, pastors were also being accused of witchcraft, and so were wealthy citizens. When even the wife of Governor William Phips was accused of being a witch, the governor was persuaded by a delegation of pastors to call off the witchcraft trials.

Often, Europeans like to point to this as an example of the ignorance and superstition of Americans. Only in America, they claim, could something like this happen, because only in America are people so prejudiced and

---

[93]Peter J. Marshall, Jr., and David B. Manuel, Jr., *The Light and the Glory* (Grand Rapids: Fleming H. Revell, 1977), 235-238.

[94]Von Rohr, 146.

intolerant. But they overlook the fact that in the same year, 1692, in which twenty people were hanged for witchcraft in Massachusetts, hundreds more were executed for the same supposed crime in several European countries.

One of the Salem judges, Samuel Sewall, a devout Christian, came to regret his actions. When his daughter died and his son was stillborn four years later, he became convinced that God was punishing him for having sentenced innocent people to death. He publicly repented on January 14, 1697, in a document titled "Petition Put Up by Mr. Sewall on the Fast Day," which reads in part, "Samuel Sewall . . . being sensible that as to the guilt contracted upon the opening of the late commission . . . at Salem, he . . . desires to take the blame and shame of it, asking pardon of men, and especially desiring prayers that God, who has unlimited authority, would pardon that sin. . . ."[95]

In 1712, the Massachusetts courts officially determined that the witch trials were a miscarriage of justice, and they ordered that payment be made to surviving victims and to the survivors of those who were unjustly executed.

Some people regard the "Red Scare" of the early 1950's as a repeat of the Salem witch trials. However, serious historians know that there was danger from Communists both within and outside our borders in those days, and that most of those who were accused in that time of membership in the Communist Party had in fact been members of the Communist Party.

A more fitting and more recent parallel would be the "Satanic ritual abuse" scare of the early 1980's, when people were accused once again on the evidence of children. In this case, it was not "spectral evidence," but "repressed memories" supposedly brought out by hypnosis. This happened not only in New England, but also in California, Minnesota, Washington State, and England. As was the case in Salem, all or almost all of the accused appear to have been innocent. So we cannot cavalierly dismiss the witch trials as an artifact of a previous day.

---

[95]Marshall and Manuel, *Light and Glory*, 238.

December 26, 2010
Christmas

Do you ever wonder how the early Congregationalists celebrated Christmas? The answer is simple: they didn't!

John von Rohr reports that it was not until 1918 that the Congregational churches even began to recognize the Christian Year at all. He says, "Seventeenth-century Congregationalists had firmly rejected as 'papist' all honoring of special religious days, except for the Sabbath, as well as all observing of special religious seasons. Even Christmas and Easter initially suffered this repudiation through Puritan conviction and determination."[96]

When the Pilgrims were still back in Holland, according to George Willison, Pastor John Robinson had expressed the opinion that "the Dutch could not possibly be true Christians so long as they went on benightedly celebrating Easter and Christmas, for which there was no warrant in Scripture."[97] Robinson even wondered why anyone would celebrate the birth of the Savior without also celebrating His circumcision.

Captain Jones of the *Mayflower* observed Christmas in 1620, when the ship was still off Cape Cod. Willison records that "on board that evening there was a little Christmas cheer, thanks to the skipper, who as a good Church of England man did not share the Saints' scruples and broke out a barrel of the ship's beer, inviting the Pilgrims to drink with him and his mates, as his guests appreciatively noted."[98]

By Christmas of 1622, many newcomers who were emphatically not Congregationalists had come to Plymouth Colony. Nathaniel Philbrick writes, "The differences between the newcomers and [the original Separatists from Leiden] came to a head on December 25. For the Pilgrims, Christmas was a day just like any other; for most of the Strangers from the [ship] *Fortune*, on the other hand, it was a religious holiday, and they informed Bradford that it was 'against their consciences' to work on Christmas. Bradford begrudgingly gave them the day off and led the rest of the men out for the usual day's work.

---

[96]Von Rohr, 436.

[97]Willison, 104.

[98]Ibid., 160-161.

But when they returned at noon, they found the once placid streets of Plymouth in a state of joyous bedlam. The Strangers were playing games, including stool ball, a cricketlike game popular in the west of England. This was typical of how most Englishmen spent Christmas, but this was not the way the members of a pious Puritan community were to conduct themselves. Bradford proceeded to confiscate the gamesters' balls and bats. It was not fair, he insisted, that some played while others worked. If they wanted to spend Christmas praying quietly at home, that was fine by him; 'but there should be no gaming or reveling in the streets.' "[99] (By the way, it seems that "stool ball" was an early form of baseball. Baseball is apparently an older American tradition than we knew.)

Before long, celebrating Christmas was no longer merely against etiquette, but against the law. Massachusetts Bay Colony's General Court issued this decree on May 11, 1659: "For preventing disorders, arising in several places within this jurisdiction by reason of some still observing such festivals as were superstitiously kept in other communities, to the great dishonor of God and offense of others; it is therefore ordered by this court and the authority thereof that whosoever shall be found observing any such day as Christmas or the like, either by forbearing of labor, feasting, or any other way, upon any such account as aforesaid, every such person so offending shall pay for every such offense five shillings as a fine to the county."[100]

By 1681, the ban on keeping Christmas was revoked, though most Congregationalists still did not celebrate it. One writer lamented that many people in New England were now celebrating Christmas, but he added the comment, "Blessed be God! No Authority yet [compels] them to keep it."[101] It is hard to say when most Americans began celebrating Christmas, but it is recorded that Congress was in session on December 25, 1789; and as late as 1847, no New England college took a Christmas break. Christmas did not become a Federal holiday until 1870.

---

[99]Philbrick, 128.

[100]"When Christmas Was Banned in Boston," *Massachusetts Travel Journal* « http://masstraveljournal.com/comment/116» (accessed 27 Apr 2012).

[101]"Christmas a Crime," *Celebrate Boston* «http://www.celebrateboston.com/crime/puritan-christmas-law.htm» (accessed 27 Apr 2012).

January 2, 2011
Cotton Mather

Before we finally leave the seventeenth century, I thought it would be good to look at the life of Cotton Mather. Mather was born in 1663 in Boston, and he died in 1728 in Boston. He lived in Boston all his life. His father, Increase Mather, was a famous Congregational pastor, and so was his grandfather John Cotton, after whom he was named. Cotton Mather became a minister in the same Boston church, known as Second Church, that his father served.

Often when people malign Puritans, they point to men like Cotton Mather as emblems of ignorance and superstition and intolerance. As to the allegation of ignorance, it should be pointed out that Cotton Mather earned two degrees from Harvard. He was a member of the Royal Society in London, and he was given an honorary degree from the University of Aberdeen in Scotland. Regarding the allegation of superstition, it should be noted that he was a scientist. According to Clarence Carson, Cotton Mather advocated inoculation for smallpox,[102] which would still be a radical idea a century later during the lifetime of John Adams. Carson also tells us that in his book *Christian Philosophy*, among other things Mather explained Isaac Newton's physics.[103] And to challenge the allegation of intolerance, it should be pointed out that—as most Christians know experientially—the strictest Christians in terms of fidelity to the Bible both in word and in deed are the persons who know best how easy it is to slip into sin, and thus are often the most understanding of those who have fallen.[104] While they are not likely to say, "It's all right. It's no big deal"; they would agree with Jesus when He said, "Neither do I condemn you. Go, and sin no more."

Another of Mather's books was called *Magnalia Christi Americana*, an account of God's miracles in the New England colonies. Several anecdotes are given describing God's special intervention for children. Here is one of

---

[102]Clarence B. Carson, *A Basic History of the United States* (Wadley: American Textbook Committee, 1983), vol. 1, p. 130.

[103]Ibid., 135.

[104]Marshall and Manuel, *Light and Glory*, 172: "For once you really *knew* how corrupt your own nature was at its core, you would be much more inclined to readily forgive the sinfulness of others."

them: "For instance, an honest carpenter being at work upon a house where eight children [were playing] on the floor below, he let fall accidentally . . . a bulky piece of timber just over these little children. The good man, with inexpressible agony, cried out, 'O Lord, direct it!' and the Lord did so direct it, that it fell on end in the midst of the little children and then canted along the floor between two of the children, without touching one of them. But the instances of such things would be numberless."[105]   Sadly, only two of Mather's fifteen children would survive him. On October 3, 1695, he was praying for his four-year-old daughter Mary, who was very ill: "I was unaccountably assured . . . that this child shall be happy forever [and] that I and mine should be together in the Kingdom of God, world without end." Three days later, she went to heaven, and Peter Marshall, Jr., reports that the epitaph on her tombstone said, "Gone but not lost."[106]

Clarence Carson writes, "Among the largest of the private libraries [was that] of Cotton Mather of Boston. . . . Mather . . . had a library of close to 4,000 titles, and his writings are filled with classical allusions, which attests to the fact that he had consulted many of them."[107]   Peter Marshall, Jr., observes, "Despite all his writing (and he authored more than 450 books, tracts, and treatises), he made a point of always being available to anyone in need, and he instituted what was to become an American pastoral tradition: regular calls on his aged and ailing parishioners, as well as prisoners."[108]

Mather had very advanced ideas for his time. A controversy developed over the new idea of putting musical notes into hymnals. Mather was in favor of the change. He preached the ordination sermon for a Baptist minister in 1718, and he advocated unity among all true Christian churches, whether they were Congregational or Baptist or Presbyterian. John von Rohr says, "He gave extensively of his own salary to the needy, administered gifts bequeathed for charitable purposes . . . organized societies for good works and developed charity hospitals and schools."[109]

---

[105]Ibid., 210.

[106]Ibid., 176.

[107]Clarence Carson, vol. 1, p. 125.

[108]Marshall and Manuel, *Light and Glory*, 176.

[109]Von Rohr, 178.

Mather kept praying for revival. The Great Awakening began six years after his death.

January 9, 2011
The Saybrook Platform

As promised, we are finally leaving the seventeenth century behind in our weekly discussions of Congregationalism. Most histories of our movement seem to jump right from the 1600's into the 1800's, with hardly a glance at anything in between—except, in some cases, for the Great Awakening. A researcher looking for information about eighteenth-century Congregationalism feels almost like an archeologist or a paleontologist. But we will attempt to find as much as we can about the eighteenth century.

The earliest significant development in that century was the Saybrook Platform. This resulted from a feeling among Congregational leaders that the movement had seriously declined. In England, the Anglican Church had been re-established, and in New England the people had become lukewarm. Williston Walker says, "It was with pathetic, almost exaggerated, consciousness of their own comparative feebleness that the ecclesiastical writers of the second and third generations looked back to the giants of the early days. . . . To the majority of the ministers of the time the outlook seemed full of peril."[110] One result of this concern was the publishing of the Proposals of 1705 by the assembled Congregational ministers of Massachusetts, which would in turn inspire the Saybrook Platform in Connecticut.

There was a concern that many churches calling themselves Congregational were no longer truly congregational in polity, but really Presbyterian. One Congregational church even received a pastor who had been ordained by a Presbyterian synod. The Proposals were sixteen in number. The first was "That the ministers of the country form themselves into associations that may meet at proper times to consider such things as may properly lie before them relating to their own faithfulness towards each other and the common interest of the churches. . . ."[111] Briefly, the idea was that the churches associated together would certify the qualifications of Congregational ministers, that they would adjudicate disputes between member churches, and that they would judge cases where it was alleged that a local church had departed from Congregationalism, or even from Christian orthodoxy.

---

[110]Walker, 466.

[111]Ibid., 487.

In 1708 the Saybrook Synod in Connecticut created a platform that, even though it was the product of a meeting of Congregational ministers, was taken up and enacted into law by the General Court of Connecticut. The platform contained fifteen points, including these: ". . . The elder or elders of a particular church with the consent of the brethren of the same have power and ought to exercise church discipline . . . in relation to all scandals that fall out within the same. And it may be meet in all cases of difficulty for the respective pastors of particular churches to take advice of the elders of the churches of the neighborhood before they proceed to censure in such cases. ... The churches which are neighboring each to other shall consociate for the mutual affording of each other such assistance as may be requisite. . . . The particular pastors and churches within the respective counties in this government shall be one consociation. . . . All cases of scandal that fall out within the circuit of any of the aforesaid consociations shall be brought to a council of the elders and also messengers of the churches within the said circuit. . . . When any case is orderly brought before any council of the churches it shall there be heard and determined, which . . . shall be a final issue. . . . If any pastor and church doth obstinately refuse . . . the determination of the council . . . the sentence of non-communion shall be declared against such pastor and church. . . ."[112]

Here is the paradox at the heart of our movement: all churches are to be independent, yet all are to agree on core beliefs about the church. This is impossible, humanly speaking, and obviously requires the intervention of the Holy Spirit. John von Rohr comments about the Saybrook Platform: "Opponents protested its presbyterianizing tendencies. . . . The Saybrook Platform was quietly dropped from the colony's laws in 1784."[113]

---

[112]Ibid., 503-504.

[113]Von Rohr, 136, 226.

January 16, 2011
John Wise

Last week, we looked at the Saybrook Platform of 1708. This week, we will talk about John Wise, pastor of the Second Parish Church in Ipswich, Massachusetts, one of the most outspoken opponents of that platform. Like other opponents, Wise felt that the platform gave too much power to synods or consociations that were set above the local church. He believed that this went against what he saw as the very heart of Congregationalism, the independence and sufficiency of the local church. "An Adventure in Liberty," a pamphlet published by our National Association, puts it this way: "In 1710 John Wise wrote his first essay, *The Church's Quarrel Espoused*. It constituted a protest against the attempts made by Cotton and Increase Mather to place the Massachusetts churches under the authority of ecclesiastical councils. Perceiving a reactionary revolution in the movement begun by the Mathers, he answered forcefully and brilliantly in this essay and successfully dealt a death blow to the movement."[114]

Wise first came to prominence in the late 1680's, during the time of Governor Andros, who had been appointed by King James II to bring New England to heel under one central government. There was considerable opposition to this. John von Rohr records, "Most courageous was the town of Ipswich, which, under the leadership of its minister John Wise, refused to pay any of the new taxes. Wise, who has been called 'the first great American democrat,' developed a political philosophy early in his public life that stressed the natural rights of the individual and the formation of government by social contract. Rejecting all forms of monarchy and aristocracy, he affirmed that political power rests solely with the people and that political decisions must be made by popular vote. In the struggle with Andros this meant 'no taxation without representation,' a position in which Wise anticipated the later protests of the American Revolution by more than seventy-five years. For his resistance to colonial authority, however, Wise was imprisoned, fined, and temporarily suspended from his ministry."[115]

---

[114]Gaius Glenn Atkins and Helen E. Phillips, *An Adventure in Liberty: A Short History of the Congregational Christian Churches* (Oak Creek: National Association of Congregational Christian Churches, 1990), 17-18.

[115]Von Rohr, 131-132.

Sydney Ahlstrom comments, "So clearly did [Wise] anticipate later revolutionary attitudes that his tracts were republished in the 1770s to bolster the Patriot cause."[116]

John von Rohr is worth quoting again, in his description of Wise's best-known booklet: "In 1717 his major writing appeared, a treatise titled *Vindication of the Government of New England Churches.* The vindication, however, was based not on biblical authorization, but on a conviction that 'the light of nature' dictates the superiority of democratic government, whether it be in the state or in the churches. Within the state it commends a 'compact' form of government that recognizes all persons as free and equal. . . . Similarly, Wise said, this reasoning applies in the church where democracy can be seen as superior to either monarchy or aristocracy, for here too the light of nature urges that 'power is originally in the people.' Christ, Wise added, surely was aware of this, and if he 'settled any form of power in his church,' it must have been that which exposes the members in least fashion to arbitrary measures inflicted by others. So on these grounds, fashioned by reason's perception of natural rights, democracy for Congregationalism and the autonomy of its local churches must be maintained."[117]

I have a reprint of the booklet, and it is interesting how Wise frankly admits that he is guided by logic rather than Scripture, while realizing that he at least must tip his hat to the Bible: speaking of the Congregational Way, he says, "And certainly it is agreeable that we attribute it to God whether we receive it nextly from reason or revelation, for that each is equally an emanation of His wisdom, *Prov. 20. 27*: 'The spirit of man is the candle of the Lord, searching all the inward parts of the belly.' There be many larger volumes in this dark recess called the belly to be read by that candle God has lit up." He goes on to identify this "candle" with the light of Christ: "This admirable effect of Christ's creating power in hanging out so many lights to guide man through a dark world is as applicable to the light of reason as to that of revelation."[118]

---

[116] Ahlstrom, 351.

[117] Von Rohr, 160.

[118] John Wise, *A Vindication of the Government of New-England Churches*, 25, in Larson.

January 23, 2011
Edward Taylor

Some of you know that I am a poet, so naturally I am interested when I read about a poet I never heard of before, and I become especially interested when I find that he—like me—was a Congregational minister. Edward Taylor was born in Sketchley, Leicestershire, England, in 1642. In 1668, he emigrated to Massachusetts. He was married twice, and altogether he was the father of fourteen children, though five of them died in childhood. In 1679, Taylor became pastor of the Congregational church in Westfield, Massachusetts, which was then on the frontier between civilization and wilderness. He remained pastor there for fifty years, until his death in 1729. Taylor had about two hundred books in his personal library, many of them copied by hand because he could not afford to buy the originals. He wrote many sermons, of course, and also many books and tracts on theological matters. Conservative in his theology, he was a fierce opponent of Jonathan Stoddard's view that anyone—believer or not, unrepentant sinner or not—was eligible to take Communion. But Taylor is mainly remembered today for his poetry. When he died, his grandson was his heir, and the grandson, Ezra Stiles (who would later be president of Yale), honored Taylor's wish that his poems not be published. In fact, none of them were ever published until 1939, and a complete collection of his poetry was not published until 1960. He has been called "colonial America's greatest poet."[119]

"Housewifery" is described in a couple of sources as Taylor's best-known poem. Here are the first six lines:

Make me, O Lord, Thy spinning wheel complete.
Thy Holy Word my distaff make for me.
Make mine affections Thy swift flyers neat
And make my soul Thy holy spool to be.
My conversation make to be Thy reel
And reel the yarn thereon spun of Thy wheel.

In a poem called "The Reflection," Taylor describes his vision of Jesus Christ at the Communion table:

---

[119]"Edward Taylor," Answers.com « http://www.answers.com/topic/teddy-taylor» (accessed 28 Apr 2012).

Once at Thy feast, I saw Thee pearl-like stand
'Tween heaven and earth, where heaven's bright glory all
In streams fell on Thee, as a floodgate, and
Like sunbeams through Thee on the world to fall.

Here are some lines from Taylor describing the ascension of Christ:

God is gone up with a triumphant shout,
The Lord with sounding trumpets' melodies.
Sing praise, sing praise, sing praises out,
Unto our King sing praises seraphic-wise.
"Lift up your heads, ye lasting doors,"
They sing, "and let the King of Glory enter in."

Here is a triumphant poem celebrating Jesus' victory over death and sin:

Infinity's fierce fiery arrow red
Shot from the splendid bow of Justice bright
Did smite Thee down, for Thine. Thou art their Head.
They died in Thee. Their death did on Thee light.
They died their death in Thee. Thy death is theirs.
Hence Thine is mine. Thy death my trespass clears.
How sweet is this: my death lies burièd
Within Thy grave, my Lord, deep underground.
It is unskinned, as carrion rotten, dead.
For Grace's hand gave Death its deadly wound.
Death's no such terror on the saints' blessed coast.
It is but a harmless shade: no walking ghost.[120]

---

[120]"Poets of Cambridge, U.S.A."
«http://www.harvardsquarelibrary.org/poets/taylor.php» (accessed 28 Apr 2012).

January 30, 2011
Zabdiel Boylston

Zabdiel Boylston was a great-uncle of our second President, John Adams. None of the sources I consulted told me whether he was a member of a Congregational church, but he was associated with one of the most famous Congregational pastors, Cotton Mather. Boylston was a doctor who was born in Brookline, Massachusetts, in 1680. He never went to medical school, but he learned his profession by being apprenticed to his father, who had been trained as a physician in England. He also trained under another Boston physician. There would be no medical schools in North America until 1765.

Boylston became a very successful and wealthy physician and surgeon in Boston. He was well known among his patients, other doctors, and scientists in both America and England, for both his medical skills and his scientific research into the plants, animals, and insects of North America. He performed the first surgical operation by an American, the first removal of gallstones, and the first surgery to remove a breast tumor.

Zabdiel Boylston came to public attention during a smallpox epidemic in 1721. Smallpox evidently had come to New England in April from a ship out of the West Indies. The public was terrified. People were getting sick and dying in large numbers. Cotton Mather, according to one account, had a slave named Onesimus, who had told Mather that inoculation with infected skin was practiced in Africa in order to stimulate the body to become resistant to smallpox. Another account says that Mather got his information from two doctors in Turkey named Timoni and Pilarini. (I would prefer to believe the former account, since it is more picturesque, but usually the more routine version of a story is the true one.)

In any case, Mather distributed pamphlets to all the physicians in Boston, urging them to use inoculation against smallpox. (Mather had earlier written journal articles about smallpox inoculation in 1714-1716 that were published in England.) The doctors did not respond, so in June Mather wrote to Boylston personally. Later that month, Boylston inoculated his only son and two male slaves (Jack and Jackie). This was the first time that inoculation against smallpox was practiced in the American colonies. Boylston's son, Thomas, and the two slaves recovered from their mild case of smallpox and developed an immunity to the disease from then on. By the following February, Boylston had inoculated 241 people. Only six of them died, and four of those who died had already contracted smallpox before their inoculation. That means that 2.5 percent of those who had been inoculated died, while 14 percent died out of those who contracted the disease, not having been inoculated.

Boston's city government was against the practice. So were many of the doctors and pastors in the city. Here are some of the remarks of Boylston's opponents: "For a man to infect a family in the morning with smallpox and to pray to God in the evening against the disease is blasphemy." "Smallpox is a judgment of God on the sins of the people, and to avert it is but to provoke Him more." "Inoculation is an encroachment on the prerogatives of Jehovah, whose right it is to wound and smite."[121] "I do not see how we can be excused from great impiety herein, when ministers and people . . . have been carrying about instruments of inoculation, and bottles of the poisonous humor, to infect all who were willing to submit to it. . . ."[122]

Boylston's enemies wanted him tried for murder. His friends believed that it had become unsafe for him to go outside his house at night, so he would make house calls only after midnight, and only in disguise. Someone threw a grenade into Cotton Mather's house, both because Mather had encouraged and supported Boylston, and because Mather had allowed another pastor who had been inoculated to stay for a while at Mather's house. Things got so bad that Dr. Boylston eventually fled to England and stayed there for a year and a half before returning to Boston. He took to raising horses instead of practicing medicine, and died in 1766.

---

[121]"Zabdiel Boylston," *Today in Science History* «http://todayinsci.com/B/Boylston_Zabdiel/Boylston_Zabdiel.htm» (accessed 28 Apr 2012).

[122]"Zabdiel Boylston," *Celebrate Boston* «http://www.celebrateboston.com/biography/zabdiel-boylston.htm» (accessed 28 Apr 2012).

February 6, 2011
The Great Awakening

The Great Awakening lasted for about thirty years, from about 1726 to about 1756. This was a series of Christian revivals that stretched from Georgia to New England. The most famous preachers involved were Jonathan Edwards, a New England Congregationalist; and George Whitefield, a Calvinistic Methodist who had come over from England. The revivals were supported by many Congregational ministers other than Edwards, but they were also opposed by many other Congregationalists. To many, what was called "enthusiasm" in religion was a bad thing, seen both in the Great Awakening here in America and in the Methodist movement in England.

According to Peter Marshall, Jr., "The Great Awakening was actually a reawakening of a deep national desire for the Covenant Way of life. This yearning did not die with the passing of the Puritan era, but only went dormant. It was a desire which would produce a new generation of clergymen who would help to prepare America to fight for her life. It is a hunger so deeply engrained in the American national psyche that it can never die, although it can go fast asleep and lie dormant for years. God reawakened that desire in the 1740s—and what He has reawakened once, He can reawaken again."[123]

Jonathan Edwards wrote a book called *Narrative of Surprising Conversions*, in which he told about the conversion of a young woman in Northampton, Massachusetts, who had been one of the loosest in morals in the whole town. Edwards wrote, "God made it, I suppose, the greatest occasion of awakening to others of anything that ever came to pass in the town. I have had abundant opportunity to know the effect it had, by my private conversation with many. The news of it seemed to be almost like a flash of lightning upon the hearts of young people all over the town, and upon many others. . . . Presently upon this, a great and earnest concern about the great things of religion and the eternal world became universal in all parts of the town and among persons of all degrees and all ages. The noise of the dry bones waxed louder and louder. ... Those that were wont to be the vainest and loosest, and . . . the most disposed to think and speak slightly of vital and experimental religion, were not generally subject to great awakenings. And the work of conversion was carried on in a most astonishing manner and

---

[123]Marshall and Manuel, *Light and Glory*, 240.

increased more and more; souls did, as it were, come by flocks to Jesus Christ. . . . This work of God . . . as the number of true saints multiplied, soon made a glorious alteration in the town, so that . . . the town seemed to be full of the presence of God."[124]

This Great Awakening spread for the next couple of decades all across the American colonies, led not only by Edwards and Whitefield but by dozens of others. Whitefield became a great friend of Benjamin Franklin, who, although he was no evangelical Christian, still was persuaded by Whitefield to contribute money to the revival. Perhaps Franklin liked the boldness of men like Whitefield, who once said, "I am persuaded [that] the generality of preachers talk of an unknown and unfelt Christ. The reason why congregations have been so dead is because they had dead men preaching to them. How can dead men beget living children?"[125]

Statements like this, so common among the revivalist preachers, unsurprisingly stirred opposition among many Congregational pastors, and the Great Awakening produced a series of splits within Congregationalism. Edwards himself said that there was no middle ground, that "all must be on one side or the other."[126] Many revivalist preachers moved their churches out of the Congregational movement. Baptists were among the fiercest opponents of the Great Awakening at first, but the Baptists and the Methodists emerged as the clear winners in the struggles coming out of the revival. Congregationalism had been almost the only brand of Christianity in New England for over a century, but only a few decades after the Great Awakening had run its course, the Baptists and the Methodists would greatly outnumber the Congregationalists in America.

---

[124]William Joseph Federer, *America's God and Country: Encyclopedia of Quotations* (St. Louis: Amerisearch, 2000), 224 «http://books.google.com» (accessed 28 Apr 2012).

[125]Marshall and Manuel, *Light and Glory*, 249.

[126]Jonathan Edwards, *The Works of President Edwards* (New York: G. & C. & H. Carvill, 1830), vol. 4, p. 125 «http://books.google.com» (accessed 28 Apr 2012).

February 13, 2011
Factions in Congregationalism

We said last week that the Congregational movement was split into factions as a result of the Great Awakening. There were at least four main groups: (1) the revivalists of the Awakening themselves; (2) the "Old Side," who opposed the Great Awakening from the conservative side; (3) the "New Side," who opposed the Awakening from the liberal side, and whose main spokesman, Charles Chauncy, would lay the "foundation of later Unitarianism,"[127] according to *Webster's Guide to American History*; and (4) the new Separatists, who would reject the associational system that had grown up in American Congregationalism and return to the original separatism of the Pilgrim Fathers.

Even the names of the different groups were an area of disagreement. Jonathan Edwards lumped the "Old Side" and the "New Side" together into what he called "Old Lights," meaning anyone who was insufficiently enlightened to support the revivals. Those who agreed with him were, according to his vocabulary, the "New Lights," sometimes also called the "New Divinity" people or the "Consistent Calvinists." Edwards accused all opponents of the Awakening of being rationalistic, minimizing the importance of revelation and faith and undermining people's understanding of the sovereignty of God. And then there was Samuel Mather, son of Cotton Mather, an "Old Light" who called those who took a middle-of-the-road view by the name of "Regular Lights"; but the "Regular Lights" became more commonly known as the "Old Calvinists."

Charles Chauncy, "New Side" pastor of First Church in Boston, had no use for Edwards or Whitefield or for the Awakening, accusing its leaders of "going into other men's parishes."[128] He also opposed the emotionalism of the revival: "There is, no doubt, a good use to be made of the passions . . . but they are capable of being abused, and have actually been so; as is abundantly evident from many of the disorders prevailing in these times."[129]

---

[127]Charles Van Doren and Robert McHenry, eds., *Webster's Guide to American History* (Springfield: G. & C. Merriam Company, 1971), 36.

[128]Charles Chauncy, *Seasonable Thoughts on the State of Religion in New England* (Boston: Samuel Eliot, 1743), 50, in Larson.

[129]Ibid., 418-419.

For some, most of the revivalists were still not enthusiastic enough. These withdrew from fellowship with other Congregational churches, and they were called "Separate Congregationalists" or "Strict Congregationalists." Their worship tended to be extremely emotional. Spontaneous utterances, thought to be dictated by the Holy Spirit, were encouraged. Preachers must not prepare, but simply wait for the Spirit's guidance. An instantaneous conversion experience was seen to be the norm. These were what I called earlier "the new Separatists." Many of them would eventually join the Baptists (who, of course, themselves represented an earlier departure from the main body of Congregationalists). In Connecticut, Separatists were removed from public office, and many were put in prison or made to pay fines.

As opposition to the revivals continued, despite the fact that people sympathizing with the Great Awakening outnumbered the opponents by three to one, and despite the fact that the revivals were an ecumenical movement with support among Congregationalists and Presbyterians and Anglicans alike, Congregationalism was further weakened by the departure of many New Light Congregationalists who had never been part of the Separatist movement. Believing that the main body of Congregationalism was not fervently enough attached to the Awakening, many of these people, like the Separatists, also became Baptists.

Martin Marty writes, "Whoever wishes to find an explanation for the shift in power and the relative loss by the 'colonial big three' to the 'frontier big three,' from Congregational-Presbyterian-Episcopal dominance to Baptist-Methodist-Disciples of Christ predominance, can find much of the clue in one word: revivalism."[130] Justo González concludes, "At first, the Baptists opposed the movement, calling it frivolous and superficial. But, although the movement in its early stages was led by Congregationalists and Presbyterians, in the long run it was the Baptists and Methodists who most profited from it."[131]

---

[130]Martin Marty, "North America," in *The Oxford Illustrated History of Christianity*, ed. John McManners (New York: Oxford University Press, 1992), 395.

[131]González, vol. 2, p. 229.

February 20, 2011
Jonathan Edwards

Jonathan Edwards was a very important figure for at least three reasons: (1) He was a strong believer in the Congregational Way, trying to get Congregational churches to return to the original ideal of the "gathered church," a church composed not of mere churchgoers but of genuine believers; (2) He was one of the best-known and most effective leaders of the Great Awakening; and (3) He has been called the greatest philosopher ever produced by America. We will spend more than one of our "Congregational Minutes" on him. Today, we will begin an overview of his life.

Clarence B. Carson, noting that Edwards was born in 1703 and died in 1758, gives a thumbnail sketch of his life in very economical language: "Edwards was born in Connecticut, trained at Yale, became a Congregational minister, and was pastor of churches in New York and Massachusetts. He was the leading Calvinist thinker in 18th century America, sparked the Great Awakening in New England, and was a foremost philosopher of his time. In his later years, he became a missionary to the Indians, and in the last year of his life accepted an appointment as president of the College of New Jersey ([later known as] Princeton)."[132] Even such a sparse account makes quite an impression.

John Smith and others give a fuller account in their introduction to *A Jonathan Edwards Reader*. They tell us that Edwards was born October 5, 1703, in East Windsor, Connecticut. His father, Timothy Edwards, was also a Congregational minister. His maternal grandfather was the famous Solomon Stoddard, the Congregational minister who was the founder of "Stoddardeanism," which Edwards would oppose later in life as being too liberal a view of the church and the Sacraments. Edwards graduated from Yale and then earned his master's degree. He was briefly a pastor in Bolton, Connecticut, before he went back to Yale to serve as a tutor for two years. He made a study of the flax spider that was highly regarded.[133] Here is a short quotation from that study: "If there be not web more than enough just to equal with its levity the gravity of the spider, the spider together with the web will

---

[132]Clarence Carson, vol. 1, p. 100.

[133]Jonathan Edwards, *A Jonathan Edwards Reader*, eds. John E. Smith, Harry S. Stout, and Kenneth P. Minkema (New Haven: Yale University Press, 1995), x-xi.

hang *in equilibrio*, neither ascending nor descending, otherwise than as the air moves; but if there be so much web that its ascending tendency, or rather the buoying force of the air upon it, shall be greater than the descending tendency of the spider, they will ascend till the air is so thin, till they together are just of an equal weight with so much air."[134]   The famous historian Vernon Parrington complained that such a great scientist was wasted in the less important area of religion.

Like Saint Augustine, Jonathan Edwards was as much a philosopher as he was a theologian, and his work in epistemology and ontology is still well respected today.   He also wrote about free will, about redemption, original sin, the Trinity, and other standard theological topics.   In addition, he was a biographer and a historian.   His account of the Great Awakening was not propaganda or advertising for the movement. He recorded the excesses of the revivals (such as the gruesome suicide of one of Edwards's own uncles, who came down from the heights of religious ecstasy to the depths of doubt and depression) as well as the positive side of the Awakening. He concluded with a balanced view of the importance of the emotions and the importance of the intellect in the life of a Christian. Love for Christ and joy in Christ were just as important as holy living and correct doctrine.

Edwards was envious of his wife's spirituality, which he believed was much deeper than his own. Sarah Edwards would bear eleven children, and their relationship was a true love story. Edwards wrote very frankly about his passion for Sarah, and he was equally frank in trying to evaluate the strength of his passion for the Lord Jesus objectively, in order to continue improving spiritually. We will see next week how his zeal for a genuine Christian life for himself and for others led to his dismissal from his beloved church in Northampton, Massachusetts.

---

[134]Ibid., 4.

February 27, 2011
In the Hands of an Angry God

We continue this week with our biographical notes on Jonathan Edwards. I said last week that Edwards was very frank in writing about his love for his wife, Sarah. That was an understatement. The editors of *A Jonathan Edwards Reader* say that "his relationship with her is essential for our understanding of the beauty and almost sexual intimacy that he used to characterize the saint's relationship to Christ. Toppling modern-day assumptions about Puritan prudery, Edwards celebrates sexual attraction: 'How greatly are we inclined to the other sex!' Even more, attraction to 'fellow creatures' does not get in the way of our love to God, 'but only refines and purifies it.' "[135]

Clearly, then, despite his reputation as a serious scientist, philosopher, theologian, and psychologist, Edwards was a very passionate man. That makes it all the harder to imagine him in the pulpit. By all accounts, he would not have been considered a great preacher by the standards of today. He droned on in a monotonous voice. He never made eye contact with his congregation. He never even looked up from his written text. Apparently, even when he read the words I am about to quote from his most famous sermon, "Sinners in the Hands of an Angry God," written at the height of the Great Awakening, he spoke in his usual dull manner.

And yet the reaction was tremendously emotional, as people shrieked and wailed and swooned at these powerful words: "The God that holds you over the pit of hell, much as one holds a spider, or some loathsome insect, over the fire, abhors you, and is dreadfully provoked; his wrath towards you burns like fire; he looks upon you as worthy of nothing else but to be cast into the fire. . . you are ten thousand times so abominable in his eyes as the most hateful venomous serpent is in ours. . . . 'Tis nothing but his hand that holds you from falling into the fire every moment: 'tis to be ascribed to nothing else that you did not go to hell . . . last night. . . . And there is no other reason to be given why you have not dropped into hell since you arose in the morning, but that God's hand has held you up: there is no other reason to be given why you haven't gone to hell since you have sat here in the house of God, provoking his pure eyes by your sinful wicked manner of attending his solemn worship. . . . O sinner! Consider the fearful danger you are in: 'tis a great furnace of

---

[135]Ibid., xxxiii.

wrath, a wide and bottomless pit, full of the fire of wrath . . . you hang by a slender thread, with the flames of divine wrath flashing about it, and ready every moment to singe it and burn it asunder; and you have no interest in any mediator, and nothing to lay hold of to save yourself, nothing to keep off the flames of wrath, nothing of your own, nothing that you ever have done, nothing that you can do, to induce God to spare you one moment."[136]

So it was inside, in his heart and mind, and not in his outward manner, where the passion lay. Who knows how much this inner fire and outer impassiveness contributed to his alienation from his church in Northampton, Massachusetts. His parishioners felt that he had mishandled a case of church discipline, when some young men in the church were making obscene remarks to some of the young women. And many who had been admitted to church membership under the lax standards begun by his grandfather resented Edwards's efforts to tighten those standards, so that only true Christians could become members and take Communion. The editors of *A Jonathan Edwards Reader* comment: "The irony of . . . the internationally revered theologian being summarily dismissed by his own congregation offers compelling testimony to the power of the pew in Congregational New England. . . ."[137] Sydney Ahlstrom puts it even more poignantly: ". . . On 1 July 1750, he preached his farewell sermon, an utterance whose quiet compacted strength still proclaims the man's greatness in a tragic hour. After dedicating twenty-three years of his life to Northampton, making it for a time a famous center of orthodoxy and revived spirituality, he was set adrift with a wife and seven dependent children."[138]

---

[136]Ibid., 97-98.

[137]Ibid., xxiii.

[138]Ahlstrom, 304.

March 6, 2011
An Ironic End

We said last week that Jonathan Edwards, while inwardly passionate, tended not to show his emotions outwardly. This was not always true. Sarah Edwards told about her husband's being moved to tears by the preaching of George Whitefield, whom Edwards had invited to preach at his church in Northampton. Of course, this was before Edwards was fired by the church. We left on that sad note last week, but that was not the end of Edwards's story.

Sydney Ahlstrom writes, "Edwards was lifted from the anxieties of his expulsion by a call to Stockbridge, Massachusetts, a frontier town where . . . the Bay Colony's Board of Commissioners for Indian Affairs maintained a mission. . . . Although he also had to carry on a double ministry, to the whites and to the Indians, he now was free from many time-stealing distractions. . . . The Stockbridge years actually became the most productive in his life."[139]

Ahlstrom says admiringly, "In the long run the influence of Jonathan Edwards and the unfinished edifice of his thought is the most enduring result of the New England Awakening."[140] In a later chapter, Ahlstrom sums up the communion controversy that caused Edwards's dismissal by his church: "The membership pledge he asked for was no more rigorous than the Anglican confirmation vow. Yet he did make a decisive break with the accepted principles of Stoddardeanism, and he cast a shadow upon the Half-Way Covenant. He accepted what his Congregational colleagues were unwilling to admit—that the Holy Commonwealth and its 'national covenant' were gone, utterly dead. The church was living in a new age; it stood in a new relation to the world. He rejected the older view that New England's total corporate errand was part of God's design. His grandfather's easy identification of town meeting and church meeting was found wanting. The church, he was convinced, must be gathered out of the world. On this general point Edwards's influence, exerted through his books, sermons, and example, was decisive; and he has been called in truth 'the father of modern

---

[139]Ibid.

[140]Ibid., 287.

Congregationalism.' No works document this aspect of Edwards better than those on the problem of church communion."[141]

We have already looked at some of Edwards's theological and scientific writing. Here is a very lively excerpt from one of his philosophical works, on ontology, called "Of Being": "That there should absolutely be nothing at all is utterly impossible. . . . It puts the mind into mere convulsion and confusion to endeavor to think of such a state, and it contradicts the very nature of the soul to think that it should be; and it is the greatest contradiction . . . to say that there should not be. 'Tis true we can't so distinctly show the contradiction by words, because we cannot talk about it without speaking horrid nonsense and contradicting ourselves at every word, and because [the word] 'nothing' is that whereby we distinctly show other particular contradictions. But here we are run up to our first principle, and have no other to explain the nothingness or not being of nothing by. Indeed, we can mean nothing else by 'nothing' but a state of absolute contradiction. And if any man thinks that he can think well enough how there should be nothing, I'll engage that what he means by 'nothing' is as much something as anything that ever [he] thought of in his life; and I believe that if he knew what nothing was it would be intuitively evident to him that it could not be. So that we see it is necessary that some being should eternally be."[142]

In today's theological jargon, Edwards would be called a postmillennialist. John von Rohr tells us, "He saw the Great Awakening as the beginning of the millennium soon more fully to come and, by God's providence, commencing in America."[143]

Some aspects of Edwards's life were full of irony, including the way it ended. Here is the account, from *A Jonathan Edwards Reader*, of Edwards's death in 1758: "As a safeguard against the smallpox epidemic then prevailing in the Princeton area, Edwards, ever the student of the new science, agreed to be inoculated. Unfortunately, the serum was infected, and Edwards died on March 22."[144]

---

[141]Ibid., 305.

[142]Edwards, *Reader*, 9.

[143]Von Rohr, 244.

[144]Edwards, *Reader*, xxxviii.

March 13, 2011
The Unitarian Heresy

We said a couple of weeks ago that the Great Awakening—although it was a wonderful and mighty blessing to the Church in general, and although Congregational ministers began it and were at first its principal leaders— ended up being a disaster for the Congregational movement, with most of the new believers gravitating toward the Methodists and Baptists, and even many lifelong Congregationalists leaving for those newer denominations. This was the beginning of our great decline, from virtually the only brand of church in America to a very tiny denomination that is hardly noticed in today's United States.

An even worse disaster for the Congregational movement was the turning away of most Congregationalists from orthodox, Trinitarian Christianity to Unitarianism. Charles Singer writes, "Unitarianism came to New England as early as 1710, and by 1750 most of the Congregational ministers in and around Boston had ceased to regard the doctrine of the Trinity as an essential Christian belief. . . . The triumph of Unitarianism in New England Congregationalism seemed complete with the election of Henry Ware, an avowed opponent of the Trinitarian position, to the Hollis chair of divinity at Harvard."[145]

At first, those who would later be called Unitarians defined themselves as "rational Christians." They were children of the Enlightenment. *Rationality*, of course, is good; but *rationalism* became a rival to Biblical Christianity. The "rational Christians" rejected not only the Trinity, but virtually everything supernatural in the Bible, including the expectation of final judgment and the distinction between the saved and the lost. The Great Awakening only hastened the growth of the rational Christians, who looked at religious enthusiasm with horror and disgust. The growth of the movement continued, and it seemed really to snowball after Harvard became predominantly Unitarian in 1803. However, the word *Unitarian* was not in use in America until after an English writer coined it in 1815. William Ellery Channing, a prominent Congregational pastor, adopted the term in a sermon called "Unitarian Christianity" in 1819. And by 1825, the breakaway of the

---

[145]Charles G. Singer, "Unitarianism," in *Evangelical Dictionary of Theology*, ed. Walter A. Elwell (Grand Rapids: Baker Books, 1984), 1126-1127.

Unitarians, which had long been a reality, became official with the establishment of the American Unitarian Association.

Charles Singer explains, "In the nineteenth century, under the impact of transcendentalism, Unitarianism became steadily more radical. Its later leaders such as Ralph Waldo Emerson . . . rejected those remaining supernatural elements which William Ellery Channing had seen fit to retain."[146] While Channing was a great preacher who was still encouraging people to pray, and still preaching exclusively from the Bible, by Emerson's time Unitarianism had already drifted so far away from Biblical Christianity that in 1857, Emerson wrote a poem in honor of the Hindu god Brahma.[147]

One sad aspect of the Unitarian departure, in addition to the decimation of Congregationalism and the defection of virtually all our major preachers and our important churches, is that early Unitarians like Channing did not even seem to understand Trinitarianism. In a sermon called "Objections to Unitarian Christianity Considered," Channing said, "Trinitarianism teaches that Jesus Christ . . . and his Father . . . are strictly and literally one and the same being. . . . He who was sent into the world to save it cannot be the living God who sent him. . . . The doctrine that this Jesus was the Supreme God himself, and the same being with his Father . . . seems to us a contradiction to reason and Scripture so flagrant that the simple statement of it is a sufficient refutation."[148]

I agree that such an idea is obviously wrong. But that is not what the Bible teaches us about the Trinity. We believe in one God Who exists eternally as three persons, but the persons are distinct from each other. The Father is God, the Son is God, and the Holy Spirit is God; but the Father is not the Son, the Son is not the Holy Spirit, and the Holy Spirit is not the Father.

---

[146]Ibid., 1127.

[147]Ralph Waldo Emerson, "Brahma," in *The Literature of the American Renaissance*, ed. Rex Burbank and Jack B. Moore (Columbus: Charles E. Merrill Publishing Company, 1969), 164.

[148]William E. Channing, *Works* (Boston: George G. Channing, 1849), vol. 5, p. 395.

April 3, 2011
Successful Mergers in Our Past

When we are asked how we are different from those other churches calling themselves Congregationalist (those in the United Church of Christ), the short answer that most of us give is that our association was founded by the churches that refused to participate in the merger that formed the UCC in 1957. However, we need to recognize that *merger* has not always been a dirty word to Congregationalists. In 1871, the National Council of Congregational Churches was formed, but in 1931 we became the General Council of Congregational *Christian* Churches, and today we are the National Association of Congregational *Christian* Churches. How did the word "Christian" get added to our name? The answer is that there was a merger.

Probably the most interesting character in the history of the General Convention of the Christian Church, the denomination with which we joined, was James O'Kelly. Those of us who are refugees from the United Methodist denomination can take comfort in the fact that our Methodist heritage is preserved in our current denomination, because James O'Kelly was a Methodist pastor. According to John von Rohr, O'Kelly was "an ardent patriot in the American Revolution."[149] He was at first a lay preacher in the Methodist Episcopal Church, but he was later ordained. Because he was such a strong believer in republican government, O'Kelly thought that the rule by bishops that American Methodists had inherited from the Church of England was an inappropriate form of church government. For about twenty years, he struggled to reform the Methodist Episcopal Church, urging it to adopt a congregational polity.

Like most church establishments in Christian history, the Methodist organization refused to be reformed. At the General Conference in Baltimore in 1792, O'Kelly and his allies tried one last time, officially petitioning the Conference for a change in church government. When their petition was denied, they left the Methodist Episcopal Church and organized as the Republican Methodist Church. An article in *The Congregationalist* in December 2009, by Les Wicker and Rick Hartley, quotes O'Kelly as writing the following words: "I believe in God the Father Almighty, who by a

---

[149]Von Rohr, 390.

gracious Providence hath placed me in a free country, where I am secure from the rage of Kings and Bishops."[150]

Two years later, the Republican Methodist name was dropped. O'Kelly and his sympathizers decided that Christians should merely be called Christians. They also believed that the church should have no prescribed creeds and should be governed only by the Bible. During the same time period, some New England Baptist pastors had similar ideas. Led by Abner Jones and Elias Smith, they dropped the Baptist label and called themselves simply Christians. (Smith would become the publisher of what was said to be "the first religious newspaper published in the world,"[151] the *Herald of Gospel Liberty*, founded in 1808 in Cincinnati, Ohio.) Von Rohr reports, "Ironically, Congregationalism's merger partner in later years suffered in its New England beginnings at the hands of Congregationalism's Standing Order."[152] And in Kentucky, some Presbyterians, led by Barton W. Stone, who had participated in the Cane Ridge Revival in 1801 also took the name Christian and founded an independent presbytery, declaring that the Bible was their sole authority. By 1834, these three groups had joined together into what became known as the Christian Connexion.

These "Christian churches" had a radical ecclesiology that was very similar to that of the early Congregationalists of the sixteenth and seventeenth centuries, so a union seemed natural. By the time of the 1931 merger, the Christian Connexion (now called the General Convention of the Christian Church) had also absorbed the churches of the Afro-Christian Convention (which included many African-American Congregational churches). And the National Council of Congregational Churches had also taken in at least two other denominations, the Congregational Methodist Church in 1888 and the German Evangelical Protestant Church in 1925.

---

[150]Les Wicker and Rick Hartley, "The Christian Connexion," *The Congregationalist*, December 2009, 14.

[151]Ibid., 16.

[152]Von Rohr, 391.

April 10, 2011
No King but King Jesus!

Beginning in 1764, the American colonists formed Committees of Correspondence in resistance to the tyranny of King George III and his government. A little-known fact of our history is that one of the most popular slogans of those committees was "No king but King Jesus!"[153]

What was the role of the Congregational churches in the years leading up to the American Revolution? Most of the sources I consulted said that the Congregational pulpit was one of the main influences in leading the public to be ready for independence. It was the custom in New England well into the nineteenth century for pastors to give election sermons just before voting day. In 1765, just after the Stamp Act was passed, Andrew Eliot (a Congregational pastor in Boston) gave an election sermon. Lindsay Swift, in a book called *The Massachusetts Election Sermons*, says that Eliot "praised the British Constitution as the most perfect form of civil government. . . . [However, he] refers to Acts passed 'that seem hard on the Colonies.' He further asserts that 'there is perhaps not a man to be found among us, who would wish to be independent of our mother-country.' " According to Swift, Eliot attributed most of the agitation against the British government "to excessive drinking."[154] But John von Rohr points out that Eliot was a disciple of John Locke, and his sermon went on to portray "the Massachusetts charter as a contract between the king and the people that could, however, be jeopardized through violation of the popular rights that such a compact entailed. And were that to occur, resistance would be not only a right but also a duty, for submission to tyrannical use of power was itself a crime, an offense against both the state and all humanity."

Von Rohr continues by pointing out that Congregational pastors were "trained in covenant theology and nurtured on the conviction that New England occupied a special place in God's plan."[155] It became a very common

---

[153]Marshall and Manuel, *Light and Glory*, 267.

[154]Lindsay Swift, *The Massachusetts Election Sermons* (Cambridge: John Wilson and Son, 1897), 38 «http://www.archive.org/stream/massachusettsele00swif/massachusettsele00swif_djvu .txt» (accessed 28 Apr 2012).

[155]Von Rohr, 201.

theme in Congregational preaching to find Biblical passages that supported the drive for independence. Often, George III was compared to the Pharaoh who would not let God's people go. The common view among our preachers was that following the exodus, a Jewish republic was established, only to fall when the people demanded a king. Jonathan Mayhew of Boston preached, "God gave the Israelites a king in His anger, because they had not sense and virtue enough to like a free commonwealth [*i.e.*, a republic], and to have Himself for their King."[156] It was now time for God's American people to throw off their king and to re-establish the republic that God had ordained for them. Peter Marshall, Jr., says, "It was almost as if [the preachers] had George III in the front row of their congregations, and were trying to make him see the error of his ways. But if the King saw any of their sermons, he took no notice: Like Pharaoh . . . his heart was hard and growing harder."[157]

Sydney Ahlstrom comments, "In terms of church affiliation, the chief strength of Loyalism lay in the Anglican clergy everywhere and in the Anglican laity of the middle and northern colonies. . . . All in all, the Protestant disposition of the American people, regardless of how secularized their Puritanism had become, involved their viewing the king and English rule with suspicion."[158]

The tradition of reading the Old Testament into American history would continue for at least a generation. On July 4, 1799, Rev. Cyprian Strong preached, ". . . The Supreme Being took the United States, and raised them up to a state of independence. And, as the Egyptian nation, from out of which God took the Hebrews, was great and powerful, so it was as to the nation from which the United States were taken. . . . Our deliverance and national independence took place, like that of the Hebrews, by . . . a mighty hand and an outstretched arm. . . . Our independence merits a most grateful memorial on account of the many great . . . interpositions of Divine Providence in the establishment of it."[159]

---

[156]Marshall and Manuel, *Light and Glory*, 265.

[157]Ibid., 263.

[158]Ahlstrom, 361.

[159]Cyprian Strong, "A Discourse Delivered at Hebron at the Celebration of the Anniversary of American Independence," in *Passing the Torch of Liberty to a New Generation*, ed. Gary DeMar (Powder Springs: American Vision, 2009), 31-35.

May 1, 2011
Congregationalist Sermons 1799-1802

There is an interesting book called *Passing the Torch of Liberty to a New Generation*, published by American Vision, that is a collection of Congregational sermons from Connecticut pulpits, delivered between 1799 and 1802. Some of the earliest sermons in the collection were Fourth of July sermons, marking the twenty-third and twenty-fourth anniversaries of the Declaration of Independence. At the end of the volume are a series of miscellaneous messages, some for ordination services, one for Thanksgiving, another for a baptism, etc.

A couple of the sermons are titled "A Century Sermon," both preached to mark the beginning of the nineteenth century. Unlike the United States in 2000 and 2001, America was not confused in those days about when the century began: both messages were delivered on January 1, 1801. These were very optimistic sermons. Pastor Moses Welch of Mansfield ends his message with an invitation to choose Jesus Christ as Savior, so that, "at the close of the nineteenth century, when infidelity is sunk forever—when the wilderness of America shall become a fruitful field—when the banner of the cross shall be displayed from the Atlantic . . . to the shores of the Pacific Ocean—when the Lord shall have planted flourishing churches all over this land . . . then shall you look down from heaven and, with adoring angels, admire the works of God. Then shall you join the song of Moses and the Lamb, 'Great and marvelous are Thy works, Lord God Almighty; just and true are Thy ways, Thou King of saints!' "[160]

But the sermons in this collection that moved me most were those that were given on the occasion of George Washington's death. Washington had died in December 1799, and Pastor John Elliott preached a message in Guilford on February 22, 1800, that included these eloquent words: "The most eminent and extensive services to mankind will not save from death. This relentless and insatiable foe hath triumphed, and will continue to triumph, over the most elevated mortals. His dominion is established over all the race of Adam. The great and the small, the high and the low, the honorable and the despised, must lie down in the grave. Moses had his task assigned him in life, his sphere of usefulness allotted. The designs of heaven in preparing him to act in an extraordinary capacity being accomplished, he was removed from

---

[160]Ibid., 301.

time. Joshua, his successor, acted his part on the theatre of life, in leading the children of Israel to the quiet possession of the conquered country, and then yielded to the mighty destroyer of humankind. The same may be said of the most affluent, the most beloved, the most honored among the sons of men. Name Croesus, Solomon, or any even the most renowned princes . . . and it will be found that their earthly career was closed by the same melancholy event. The grim tyrant assaults the splendid palace with equal boldness and with equal success as the humble cottage. He is not dismayed by the ensigns of office, the regalia of courts, the elevation of ranks. These, at a single blow, he levels with the dust and buries in undistinguished ruin. Death ascends the throne and plunges headlong its high possessor. Nay, more than monarchs bow to the fatal stroke, *for Washington is fallen*! Let not the greatest of generals, the most eminent of statesmen, the most highly esteemed and most dearly beloved of men, expect to escape death, *for Washington is fallen*! Let not the man 'first in war, first in peace, and first in the hearts of his countrymen' hope to avoid the deadly arrow, *for Washington is fallen*! Since the peerless Trophy obtained on Calvary's mount, have few so splendid graced the triumph of the king of terrors! O Death! How numerous, how signal are thy victories! . . . Haughty conqueror! Why could not thy fury be appeased by the numerous victims which are constantly sacrificed at thy shrine? Why didst thou enforce thy claim upon the beloved Father of His Country? Why spread the mantle of mourning over a nation—over millions!—at a single blow? Never again shall such an opportunity be offered, such an object be presented to thy dart: and *he shall rise and live*, when *thou* art forever destroyed by the almighty power of the Prince of Peace."[161]

---

[161]Ibid., 127-128.

May 8, 2011
Lyman Beecher

We saw a few weeks ago that the Congregational churches were heavily involved in the Great Awakening under Jonathan Edwards and George Whitefield and many others. The next big Congregational name in the great tradition of revivalist preaching was Lyman Beecher.

Beecher was born in 1775, the same year that our American Revolution started. He did not come from a family of preachers; his father and grandfather were blacksmiths. But he attended Yale, and he fell under the influence of Yale's president, Timothy Dwight. Peter Marshall, Jr., says, "Dwight was instrumental in Beecher's coming to the Lord, during his junior year. 'I rose to pray and had not spoken five words before I was under as deep a conviction as ever I was in my life. The sinking of the shaft was instantaneous, I understood the law and my heart as well as I do now, or shall in the Day of Judgment, I believe. The commandment came, sin revived, and I died, quick as a flash of lightning.' At just this point, a sermon by Dwight … plunged young Beecher into despair. But Dwight, a veteran of harvesting souls as well as harrowing them, soon rescued the young man and sent him on his way to conversion."[162]

Beecher was ordained in 1799. The first church he served was a Presbyterian church, but Beecher was eventually tried for heresy by the Presbyterians. He had attacked a teaching popular among Presbyterians at the time, who said that if it was God's will for a person to go to hell, the most pious thing that person could do was to accept his fate and go there quietly and without protest. After Beecher was acquitted of the charge of heresy by the Presbyterians, he afterward served mostly in Congregational churches.

Starting in 1810 in Litchfield, Connecticut, Beecher conducted what he called "continuous revivals." According to *Webster's Guide to American History*, he would rail "at intemperance, Roman Catholicism, and religious tolerance."[163] Obviously, the editors of the *Webster's Guide* were not sympathetic to Beecher's crusade against Unitarianism. John von Rohr quotes Beecher as complaining that the Unitarians "sowed tares while men slept and

---

[162]Marshall and Manuel, *From Sea to Shining Sea* (Grand Rapids: Fleming H. Revell, 1986), 112.

[163]Van Doren and McHenry, 831.

grafted heretical churches on orthodox stumps."[164] As we learned earlier, most of the important Congregational churches and their pastors had become Unitarian, and there was a tremendous amount of heated rhetoric on both sides for about two years, until the Unitarians saw that they would not be able to shut Beecher up.

At first, Beecher was against the movement in the New England states to remove Congregationalism as their established church, but later he said, according to Von Rohr, that disestablishment was "the best thing that ever happened," because "it cut [them] loose from dependence on state support and threw them wholly on their own resources and on God."[165]

As you might expect of the father of Harriet Beecher Stowe, Beecher was fervently anti-slavery. In 1827, he preached, "Still [the flame of freedom] burns, and still the mountain heaves and murmurs; and soon it will explode with voices, and thunderings, and great earthquakes. And then will the trumpet of jubilee sound, and earth's debased millions will leap from the dust, and shake off their chains, and cry, 'Hosanna to the Son of David.' "[166]

Later, Beecher became president of Lane Seminary in Cincinnati. Despite his earlier experience, for some reason he accepted a call to a Presbyterian church there, and he was tried for heresy again, for supposedly not adhering closely enough to the Westminster Confession. Again he was acquitted, but he then retired and lived the rest of his life with one of his thirteen children, the famous Henry Ward Beecher.

America's long line of evangelistic preachers continued with another Congregationalist, Charles Finney; later, with Dwight L. Moody, also a Congregationalist; later still, with Billy Sunday, who influenced a preacher named Mordecai Ham. At one of Mordecai Ham's meetings, Billy Graham was converted. And the rest, as they say, is history.

---

[164]Von Rohr, 253.

[165]Ibid., 250.

[166]Ahlstrom, 646.

May 15, 2011
The Plan of Union

We've talked about a couple of the events that had a negative impact on the Congregational movement. There was the Great Awakening, which was a blessing to America and a triumph for the Church generally, although it resulted in fewer Congregationalists and more Baptists and Methodists; there was the Unitarian departure, which took away most of the important Congregational churches and most of our pastors. After that, the biggest fiasco for the Congregational churches (until 1957) was the Plan of Union of 1801.

Harry Butman gives a very succinct account of this episode: "The Plan of Union was a well-meant ecumenical effort which became a Congregational disaster. Briefly and crudely said, the Connecticut General Association and the General Assembly of the Presbyterian Church agreed upon a plan of missionary enterprise which gave the country west of the Hudson River to the Presbyterians while New England remained Congregational territory. In 1801 the West was a malarial, Indian-haunted wasteland. The Presbyterians boldly bet on the West and won much. The Plan of Union resulted in great gain for the Presbyterians: Dissenting Congregationalists bitterly complained, 'They have milked our Congregational cows and made Presbyterian butter and cheese.'

"As a result of strong and widespread dissatisfaction among Congregationalists concerning the Plan of Union, in 1852 a large convention of Congregational churches was held in Albany, New York. It was the first national gathering of Congregational churches in over two hundred years. It abrogated the Plan of Union and after a half-century halt, Congregationalism resumed its westward march."[167]

Virtually all Christians have yearned for true unity of the universal Church, and indeed that unity is clearly the Lord's will for His Church. Theologically, Presbyterians and Congregationalists are practically identical. However, our important difference is that in Congregationalism, each local church is considered to embody the Church in all its completeness, with no authority over it except Jesus. But every local Presbyterian church is subject to the authority of a synod or presbytery. We could not truly unite with the

---

[167]Butman, *Symbols*, 10.

Presbyterians without sacrificing our view of the church, which we consider to be true and Biblical

But of course, the Plan of Union was not truly a union of our denominations, just an agreement not to compete with each other. And in hindsight, it looks obvious that it was not advantageous to Congregationalists. In return for being allowed to hunker down in New England without competition from Presbyterians, we forfeited our right to plant new churches west of the Hudson River. At best, this was a recipe for stagnation or fossilization. At worst, it was a plan that seemed designed to result in the shrinking of our denomination.

However, some Congregationalist church planters simply ignored the Plan of Union during the half century of its existence. John von Rohr reports that Congregationalism did spread into Illinois, Michigan, Wisconsin, Minnesota, Missouri, Oregon, California, and Iowa during those years.[168] Some Presbyterian churches in Iowa even transformed themselves into Congregational churches.

Williston Walker, one of our important Congregationalist historians, says that it would be unfair to blame the Presbyterians for the consequences of the Plan of Union. He says, "The fault was chiefly Congregational. . . . If the denominational consciousness of Congregationalism was weak, that of Presbyterianism was awake and considerably assertive."[169] In the end, this ecumenical experiment left a bad taste in Congregational mouths. Pastor Nathanael Emmons of Franklin, Massachusetts, even advocated a return to separatism: "Associationism leads to Consociationism; Consociationism leads to Presbyterianism; Presbyterianism leads to Episcopacy; Episcopacy leads to Roman Catholicism. . . ."[170]

---

[168]Von Rohr, 267-271.

[169]Walker, 533.

[170]Von Rohr, 292.

May 29, 2011
Edward Beecher and Harriet Beecher Stowe

We talked a couple of weeks ago about Lyman Beecher, briefly mentioning his thirteen children. One of those thirteen was Edward Beecher, who also became a Congregational pastor in 1826, having graduated four years earlier from Yale at the head of his class at the young age of nineteen. He was born in 1803, and by the time he became an adult the issue of slavery and its abolition was raging all across the United States. Many of the abolitionist crusaders were threatened with violence or were the victims of violence. Often, the printing presses for abolitionist newspapers were destroyed. Elijah Lovejoy began his journalistic career in St. Louis, and by the time three of his printing presses had been destroyed, he had moved to Alton, Illinois. There, defending his fourth printing press against a mob, Lovejoy was assassinated in 1837.

Edward Beecher, who at the time was the first president of Illinois College, was spurred by Lovejoy's murder to join the abolitionist cause. He wrote an account of Lovejoy's life and death, and he also produced a series of articles on what he called "organic sin,"[171] articles which became very influential in moving people toward the abolitionist position. Looking back, the abolition of slavery seems the obvious thing; but in that time, it was a ferociously-debated issue, with all kinds of shades of opinion between total support for slavery and total opposition to it. (For a parallel in our time, we might think about the issue of abortion.)

Edward Beecher in later life was part of the committee that, in 1865, produced the first statement of faith since 1648 that was agreed to by all the Congregational churches in America. But even more important for us today, Edward Beecher's influence lives on in our denomination. In 1849, he founded *The Congregationalist*, our fine magazine that is still being published today. In fact, you can pick up a copy from on top of the bookshelf in the hallway as you are going toward the social hall for coffee and refreshments after the service.

Another of Lyman Beecher's famous children was Harriet Beecher Stowe, author of *Uncle Tom's Cabin*. Of course, the book is famous, and I had known about it since childhood, but I never wanted to read it because I had always assumed it would be nothing more than simple-minded

---

[171]Ahlstrom, 653.

propaganda. But after the last person living in my great-grandfather's house died, I inherited some of the books from the family library, including *Uncle Tom's Cabin*. I was surprised to find that it was well written, that the characters were mostly very believable and very well developed, with some slaveholders portrayed sympathetically and some abolitionists shown to be less than perfect, and that far from being a servile sycophant who just said, "Yes sir, Master," Uncle Tom was actually a Christ-like character who symbolically showed how the institution of slavery was in effect crucifying Jesus all over again every time someone was enslaved or a slave was abused or killed.

Lincoln's words on meeting Mrs. Stowe are well known: "So you're the little lady who started this great war."[172] But Harriet didn't see it that way. Her conviction was that God Himself had written the book, simply using her as His instrument. The book was an immediate best-seller all over the world, being translated into forty languages. Providentially, the popularity of the French translation also led to a huge demand for the Bible in France. *Uncle Tom's Cabin* was praised by such famous writers as Henry Wadsworth Longfellow, John Greenleaf Whittier, George Sand, Henry James, and Leo Tolstoy.

Harriet was an old-fashioned Congregationalist. She never attended the theater, so she presumably never saw any of the very popular stage productions of her story. She was also somewhat naïve. Although she was a New Englander, she loved the South. She thought that even Southerners would be convinced by her novel that slavery had to be outlawed forever, and that then the South would become a nearly perfect Christian society.

---

[172]Peter Bagley, "The Little Lady Who Started the War," *The Congregationalist*, August 1985, 16, in Larson.

June 5, 2011
Marcus and Narcissa Whitman

Missionary work by American Christians did not really get started in earnest until the early nineteenth century, but Congregationalists were leaders in missions from the very beginning. Marcus Whitman was born in 1802 in New York State. He was a Congregationalist, and he studied medicine and became a physician. In his early thirties, Dr. Whitman felt that the Lord was calling him into missionary work. He applied to the American Board of Foreign Missions, and the board sent him to Oregon. While the wagon train was traveling westward along the Oregon Trail, Whitman earned the friendship of the famous mountain man Jim Bridger by digging an arrowhead out of Bridger's back. The arrowhead had been there for several years, and Dr. Whitman was surprised that it had never caused an infection. Bridger answered, "Meat don't spoil in the Rockies."[173]

Halfway to Oregon, Whitman remembered some unfinished business. He went back home and married his fiancée, Narcissa. After recruiting three other people for their mission, Marcus and Narcissa left for Oregon in 1836. The trip was difficult for Narcissa, who was pregnant. At one point, in order to lighten the wagon's load, she had to throw out the trunk that contained her wedding dress. The Whitmans' daughter, Alice Clarissa, was the first child born to United States citizens in the Oregon Territory.

Dr. Whitman established a mission among the Cayuse Indians near what is now Walla Walla, Washington, but was then part of the Oregon Territory. In addition to his medical and evangelistic work, Whitman became involved in politics as well, speaking in favor of American claims to Oregon against the British. In 1842, he made the trip east to Washington, D.C., urging President Tyler to take a strong stand in favor of United States sovereignty over the Oregon Territory. During the same trip, he successfully persuaded the Mission Board not to close his mission.

Whitman's mission had much success in saving the bodies and the souls of the Cayuse Indians. He was not able to convince them to give up their nomadic lifestyle in favor of farming, but he did get at least some of the Indians to work in the mission's flour mill, sawmill, and blacksmith shop. There were many difficulties, though. Alice Clarissa died at age three. However, the Whitmans eased their sorrow by beginning the first orphanage

---

[173]Marshall and Manuel, *Sea to Sea*, 339.

in the region, taking in orphans who had come from the families of trappers and settlers, including Jim Bridger's daughter.

Other difficulties came from the Whitmans' partners in the mission, Rev. Henry Spaulding and his wife, Eliza. Before his marriage, Spalding had unsuccessfully tried to become Narcissa's husband, and he apparently had never quite gotten over his rejection; he also resented that Whitman, and not he, had been put in charge of the mission. He became so persistent in criticizing and insulting Whitman that Narcissa wrote to her father, "The man who came with us is one who never ought to have come. My dear husband has suffered more from him in consequence of his wicked jealousy, and his great pique towards me, than can be known in this world."[174]

Despite the difficulties, the mission was successful, until 1847. There was an outbreak of measles. White children responded to medical treatment, and Whitman was able to save most of their lives. But the Indians had no immunity to this white man's disease. Half the Cayuse tribe died of measles. Unfortunately, the Indians became suspicious, thinking that Whitman was more dedicated to saving white lives than to saving Indians. The Cayuse were also becoming very alarmed by the large numbers of white people moving into their territory. They attacked the mission. Marcus and Narcissa Whitman became martyrs, and eleven other white settlers were also killed.

---

[174]Ibid.

June 12, 2011
Henry Obookiah

Henry Obookiah is a name I had never heard before I read about him in a couple of old articles in *The Congregationalist* from April 1965[175] and March 1969.[176] I also found some information on the Website of a magazine called *Coffee Times*.[177] Henry's original name was Opukaha'ia, but we will call him Obookiah, as he was called by the Americans who came to know him and who gave him the first name "Henry." He was probably born on the Big Island in 1792, and when he was somewhere between ten and thirteen years old both his parents were killed in an intertribal war. Henry tried to save his baby brother; but the baby was killed, also. Henry went to live with his uncle, a kahuna who began training Henry to become a kahuna as well. But Henry, being an orphan, was unhappy and started thinking about leaving Hawaii.

In about 1807, Henry talked his way aboard an American ship called the *Triumph*. After a long time at sea, sailing across the Pacific Ocean more than once, to the Indian Ocean, around the Cape of Good Hope and across the Atlantic, Henry found himself in New York in 1809. The ship's captain then took Henry to live with him and his family in New Haven, Connecticut.

Tutored by a Yale student named Edwin Dwight (son of Yale's president), Henry learned quickly to read English. Henry began to read enthusiastically, and he began to see that the "gods" of Hawaii were like the idols ridiculed by the prophet Isaiah. They were made of wood, the same wood that people used to warm their homes and cook their food. People created the Hawaiian "gods," but the true God had created people. A little later, Henry began living with the Dwight family, a family that prayed both mornings and evenings.

Working on farms in Connecticut and New Hampshire, Henry became well acquainted with the New Englanders. He listened to them, and this boy

---

[175]W. Lee Roddy, " 'My Betsy,' Missionary Wife," *The Congregationalist*, April 1965, 4-5, in Larson.

[176]"From Hawaii to Connecticut," *The Congregationalist*, March 1969, 10-11, in Larson.

[177]Betty Fullard-Leo, "Henry Opukaha'ia, the Youth Who Changed Hawaii," *Coffee Times*, Fall 1998 «http://www.coffeetimes.com/henry.htm» (accessed 28 Apr 2012).

who had trained for the kahuna priesthood now spoke to the farmers about his new faith in Jesus. And in his spare time, he was always studying. Churches in the Litchfield, Connecticut, area often asked him to speak in their worship services. Henry began translating the Bible into Hawaiian and also began writing a dictionary and grammar of the Hawaiian language. He attended classes at Yale, studying Latin, Hebrew, geometry, and geography, and he finished writing his autobiography in 1815.

By 1817, Henry was enrolled in the Foreign Mission School that was organized by the Congregationalists who had formed the American Board of Commissioners of Foreign Missions. The school's stated aim was to provide "education in our country of heathen youths, in such a manner as, with subsequent professional instruction, will qualify them to become missionaries, physicians, schoolmasters or interpreters, and to communicate with heathen nations such knowledge in agriculture and the arts as may prove the means of promoting Christianity and civilization."[178]

A year later, Henry was ready to return to Hawaii. But he fell ill with what a doctor diagnosed as typhus. Despite the best medical treatment that was available at the time, Henry died on February 17, 1818. It was said that he died with a beautiful smile on his face and that his last words were "Aloha oe."[179] While he had been at the Foreign Mission School, Henry greatly impressed a seminary student named Hiram Bingham. When he heard that Henry Obookiah had died, Bingham remembered hearing Henry's prayers for Hawaii. By the next year, Hiram Bingham had been ordained as a Congregational pastor. He had decided to go to Hawaii in Henry's place; and on October 23, 1819, Rev. and Mrs. Hiram Bingham and twelve other missionaries sailed on the ship *Thaddeus* for Hawaii. Their arrival in 1820 was the beginning of the conversion of the Hawaiian Islands.

Missionaries would finish Henry's work on the Bible, dictionary, and grammar. Henry Obookiah, the first Hawaiian Christian, was buried in Cornwall, Connecticut. In 1993, his body was taken back to the Big Island of Hawaii and reinterred there.

---

[178]"From Hawaii to Connecticut," 10.

[179]Fullard-Leo, "Henry Opukaha'ia."

July 3, 2011
Prayer in a Haystack

"The Haystack Prayer Meeting" is a funny-sounding name, but it identifies a very important event in Congregational history, in Christian history, in U.S. history, and in the history of the missions movement. Last time, we talked about Henry Obookiah. Besides Hiram Bingham, another Congregational student who was influenced by Obookiah was Samuel Mills. The booklet put out by our National Association titled *An Adventure in Liberty* has this to say: "American missions, both home and foreign, owe more to Samuel J. Mills than to any other one person in American religious history." He and a group of other young men at Williams College had formed a prayer group, called "the Brethren," that met on Saturday afternoons in a grove of maple trees. One Saturday in August 1806, there was a driving thunderstorm, and the young men ducked into a haystack for cover against the rain. There, Mills suggested that they ought to go to Asia to preach the Gospel. The booklet concludes, "That meeting was, in event and purpose, the birth-meeting of American Protestant foreign missions."[180]

Mills and his friends went on to Andover Seminary, and they persisted in their dream of evangelizing Asia. The Andover faculty, and other Congregational leaders, listened to these young men. In 1810, the American Board of Commissioners for Foreign Missions was established. There was some opposition to forming the board: Harry Butman reports that one opponent "objected to the export of religion when we had so little of it for domestic consumption."[181] Sydney Ahlstrom records that this was countered by a supporter who said that "religion is a commodity of which the more we exported the more we had remaining."[182] On February 8, 1812, Samuel Mills and his four friends from the Haystack Meeting—Gordon Hall, Adoniram Judson, Samuel Newell, and Samuel Nott—were ordained, and by the end of that month, some of them were on their way to India. However, by the time they got there, two of the men—one of them Adoniram Judson—had left

---

[180] Atkins and Phillips, 21.

[181] Butman, *Lord's Free People*, 50.

[182] Ahlstrom, 424.

Congregationalism to become Baptists. Those men helped the Baptist denomination to organize its own foreign-mission board in 1814.

Samuel Mills was not able to go on the journey to India, being in very poor health. He went into home mission work out on the frontier. None of the sources I consulted addressed this question, but when we think of the state of the American frontier in 1812, we might wonder whether going to India would have been any more dangerous than working out in the American West! Mills was distressed by the lack of faith among so many of the pioneers, and by the shortage of churches and pastors and even Bibles. The work of Mills on the frontier, in partnership with a Presbyterian named John Schermerhorn, would eventually lead to the formation of the interdenominational American Home Missionary Society in 1826. Mills, along with Lyman Beecher and others, in 1816 was one of the founders of the American Bible Society, which still exists today and has been very influential in spreading the Gospel to the farthest parts of the world. (If you have ever read the Good News Bible or the Contemporary English Version, you know some of the work of the American Bible Society.)

Arthur Rouner, Jr., comments, "The people of [the Congregational] Way have been free to respond to any human need that touched their hearts. ... Where the Spirit has led, we have been free to follow. . . . In the year 1806, five young men . . . took shelter under the nearest haystack. Exactly what happened there we cannot be sure. But we do know that under that haystack in the driving rain of that day a prayer-meeting took place which was to send those boys to the ends of the earth as America's first foreign missionaries. They were only college students, but they gave America both her first Board of Foreign Missions and her first Bible Society! The Holy Spirit could lead those young Congregationalists because they were free to follow."[183] Sydney Ahlstrom observes, "In countless ways the Haystack Prayer Meeting continued to have repercussions throughout the world."[184]

---

[183]Rouner, *Congregational Way*, 80.

[184]Ahlstrom, 424.

July 17, 2011
Horace Bushnell

The fact that many people regard Congregationalism as a theologically liberal movement, even though it began as quite the opposite, is due largely to a few of our nineteenth-century leaders. One of these was Horace Bushnell. Professor James Sawyer calls him the "American Congregational minister recognized as the father of American theological liberalism."[185] Born in 1802, Bushnell intended to be a lawyer until he was converted to faith in Jesus. (Mark Noll writes, "Bushnell was converted in part through the influence of Samuel Taylor Coleridge's writings."[186] Many of you know Coleridge as an English Romantic poet and friend of William Wordsworth. You may not know that despite their youthful radicalism and rejection of Christianity, both Wordsworth and Coleridge became strong Christians in their later years, and Coleridge even became an ordained minister.)

Bushnell studied at Yale Divinity School, and for more than a quarter of a century he was pastor of North Church in Hartford, Connecticut. Beginning with the idea that all language at its base is metaphorical and poetic, Bushnell taught that all statements concerning Christian doctrine were relative in nature, so that no one ought to try to convince anyone else of the literal truth of any teaching through the inadequate vehicle of human language.

Apparently, Bushnell's relativism was not all-encompassing. In 1847, he spoke about the dangers facing Congregational churches at the time, naming one of those dangers as what he called "Romanism"—in other words, Roman Catholicism. John von Rohr comments, "Burgeoning immigration was bringing new Catholic inhabitants, and the Roman Church was viewed as an autocratic power seeking domination in the New World."[187] In Bushnell's mind, this was the main reason that Americans ought to establish and support public schools, as an antidote to what was considered the harmful influence of Catholic parochial schools.

---

[185]M. James Sawyer, *Biographies of Theologians Significant in Doctrinal Development* (San Jose: By the author, 1996), 20.

[186]Mark A. Noll, "Bushnell, Horace," in Elwell, 181.

[187]Von Rohr, 266.

Bushnell believed that right action was more important than right belief. (However, he did not seem to notice the inconsistency of taking this position while at the same time being so stridently anti-Catholic!) Although he is regarded as an important theologian, Bushnell sounds more like an "anti-theologian." He rejected all the commonly-accepted theories about why Jesus had to die on the cross and what His death accomplished. In Bushnell's view, the moral example of Jesus' self-giving was in itself enough to heal people of sinful attitudes and to lead them to a saving faith. This sounds very liberal indeed to many of us, but Bushnell clearly loved Jesus with all his heart. When some of his church members complained that he talked about Jesus too much, Bushnell denied that this was "a fault to be repented of, for Christ is all and beside him there is no gospel to be preached or received."[188]

Too much intellectualism in the Church, however, *was* a fault to be repented of, in Bushnell's view. He saw the Congregational churches of New England in general as places where people went on a Sunday to be excessively solemn, as if joyful worship were not proper, and to hear a sermon that was really more like a doctrinal lecture than an invitation to live the Gospel. However, he also rejected the emotion-driven revivalism of the time, seeing it as too subjective and too individualistic. Christianity, for Bushnell, should stress the corporate nature of the Church and the command of Jesus to love one another as He has loved us.

Charges of heresy were leveled at Bushnell by other Congregational pastors, and in order to protect their pastor from having to answer such charges formally, the people of North Church left their local association and became independent. Although Bushnell is so often regarded as a leading figure in theological liberalism, his views continued to develop as he grew older, and eventually he dropped his almost Unitarian view of God and came to a more orthodox understanding of the Trinity. He does not seem to have accepted the label that has been attached to him, understanding himself as a believer who had a passionate and controlling love for Jesus.

---

[188]Ibid., 290.

July 31, 2011
Henry Ward Beecher

The most famous of Lyman Beecher's thirteen children was Henry Ward Beecher. Doesn't the name just roll grandly off the tongue? *Henry Ward Beecher!* The great Charles Spurgeon was called "the Prince of Preachers" in England, but Harry Butman insists that Henry Ward Beecher outranked Spurgeon: he calls Beecher "the emperor of American preachers."[189]

Born in 1813, Beecher grew up to be a Congregational minister like his father. He was blessed physically with a large body, a dignified manner, an impressive if not handsome face, a dynamic personality, and a powerful voice that, in Butman's words, "could roar and purr."[190] His ministerial career began in Kansas, where he raised money in his church to buy what were called "Beecher's Bibles"—rifles for the abolitionist cause. He and his brother-in-law once rescued a free black woman from slave traders. After pastoring for a while in Indianapolis, he became famous as the pastor of Plymouth Church, a Congregational fellowship in Brooklyn, New York.

Plymouth Church was a very wealthy and influential church. Famous abolitionists like William Lloyd Garrison and others spoke there. Charles Dickens read from his novels in the church building. President Lincoln and President Grant, happy that Beecher was a Republican, both attended services at Plymouth Church. Beecher himself gave at least fifty public lectures every year, in addition to preaching on Sundays. As the saying went, if you wanted to hear Beecher, "Just take the ferry to Brooklyn and follow the crowd."[191]

Beecher also wrote books. John von Rohr reports, "In 1855 he published his *Plymouth Collection of Hymns and Tunes*, which he claimed were 'wide enough in range to be used by any evangelical church.' The music was drawn from secular as well as religious sources, one of the tunes being the popular political ditty 'Tippecanoe and Tyler Too.' "[192]

---

[189]Butman, "Henry Ward Beecher: Emperor of American Preachers," *The Congregationalist*, April 1987, 4, in Larson.

[190]Ibid., 5.

[191]Marshall and Manuel, *Sounding Forth the Trumpet* (Grand Rapids: Fleming H. Revell, 1999), 261-262.

[192]Von Rohr, 300.

Science and religion must not be enemies, insisted Beecher. He was convinced that Charles Darwin was correct, and he called himself "a cordial Christian evolutionist."[193] He also minimized the authority of the Bible. In his words, "It is the human race that has been inspired; and the Bible in every part of it was lived, first, and the record of it made afterwards."[194] Unlike his father, who was a solid Calvinist, Beecher rejected the theology of the Westminster Confession. By 1882, because of so much criticism from other Congregational ministers, Beecher led his church out of the Congregational denomination into independency.

Oddly enough, Beecher's theological liberalism was not matched by what in our time would be called political liberalism. Like many other nineteenth-century thinkers, he applied Darwinism to political science and economics. He believed in the survival of the fittest, and that those who were poor deserved their lowly condition. In his words, "No man in this land suffers from poverty unless it be more than his fault—unless it be his sin. . . . If men have not enough, it is owing to the want of . . . industry, and frugality, and wise saving."[195]

Unfortunately, Beecher was alleged to have fallen into temptation. He was accused of committing adultery with the wife of one of his church members, and the resulting alienation-of-affection lawsuit became a big story in the American press, the English press, and the European press. Many books were written about the scandal, but Beecher won the court case. Plymouth Church also voted that he was innocent, and two ecclesiastical councils found him not guilty, as well. According to Harry Butman, the first of these councils had representatives from 119 churches; and at the second, 175 churches were represented.[196]

---

[193]Ibid., 323-324.

[194]Henry Ward Beecher, *A Treasury of Illustration*, eds. John R. Howard and Truman J. Ellinwood (New York: Fleming H. Revell Company, 1904) «http://www.ebooksread.com/authors-eng/henry-ward-beecher/a-treasury-of-illustration-cee/» (accessed 29 Apr 2012).

[195]Von Rohr, 328.

[196]Butman, "Emperor of American Preachers," 6.

Maybe you first heard of Beecher the way I did as a boy, in these words from Oliver Wendell Holmes, Sr.:

The Reverend Henry Ward Beecher
Called a hen a most elegant creature.
The hen, hearing that,
Laid an egg in his hat.
And thus did the hen reward Beecher.[197]

---

[197]Butman, *Lord's Free People*, 35.

August 14, 2011
Queen Kaahumanu

This week's Congregational Minute is based on two sources: an article in the January 1966 *Congregationalist* called "Hawaii's Most Amazing Queen,"[198] and an article from the Website of *Coffee Times* magazine titled "The Woman Who Changed a Kingdom."[199] The great King Kamehameha I, who united the Hawaiian Islands into a single nation, had twenty-one wives, but Kaahumanu was his favorite. She was between ten and thirteen years old when she married the king, but by the time he died in 1819, she had become an imposing figure, six feet tall and three hundred pounds. And when Kaahumanu became regent upon the king's death, one of her first acts was to order the destruction of all idols, even though her people had worshiped these "gods" for two thousand years. She also allowed women to eat with their husbands, and she threw out the prohibition against women eating pork and bananas. After the young crown prince died, Kaahumanu became the first reigning queen of Hawaii.

There was civil war in reaction to these radical changes, but it did not last long. Kaahumanu's loyal warriors quickly crushed the rebellion. For a year, the Hawaiian people had no temples, no priests, and no gods. Providentially, the missionaries arrived in 1820, and Kaahumanu was instantly attracted to Christianity. She established churches and schools, and she fought against adultery and prostitution. When she wanted to be baptized, however, Hiram Bingham refused because, he said, she was "not yet born from above with the power of the Spirit of God."[200] In late 1824, Kaahumanu became seriously ill. Mrs. Bingham cared for her devotedly until she recovered. The experience changed Kaahumanu's heart. The Binghams were now able to write in their diaries, "She was humble in Jesus." Finally, on December 4, 1825, the queen was baptized, taking on a new name, Elizabeth.

After her baptism, Elizabeth Kaahumanu said, "Teach me to read." It took her only a few days to learn to read. When she had read the Bible, she

---

[198]Roddy, "Hawaii's Most Amazing Queen," *The Congregationalist*, January 1966, in Larson.

[199]Fullard-Leo, "The Woman Who Changed a Kingdom," *Coffee Times*, June 1998 « www.coffeetimes.com/july98.htm» (accessed 29 Apr 2012).

[200]Ibid.

announced, "The law of Jehovah is the law of the land." New laws were based on the Ten Commandments. A legal system was established, and in the first jury trial Kaahumanu herself was the judge. Infanticide was made illegal. Education was mandatory: the queen declared, "When the missionaries open schools, everyone must learn to read."[201] In those early years of Hawaiian Christianity, only Congregational churches were allowed. When Catholic missionaries arrived, they were driven out of the islands.

Kaahumanu was a fervent believer, though some said that her lifestyle was not always perfectly holy. When the missionaries first met her, she was almost naked, like all Hawaiians at the time. When Mrs. Bingham convinced the queen that she ought to dress modestly, and so should her people, she reacted like a queen. She ordered the missionary wife, "Make me a dress." Again and again, she told Mrs. Bingham, "Do it over," until she was finally satisfied and was willing to wear the dress.[202] Just as her husband had taken many wives, so she also took many husbands, despite the protests of the missionaries. She was wise in the way of politics, and she recognized that many of the Westerners who had come to the islands had another agenda. Not only did they want to bring Christianity to the natives, but many of them also wanted to gain power over them. She insisted on Hawaii's sovereignty, and she thwarted what she saw as the efforts of the white people to take over the Hawaiian kingdom.[203]

In Kawaiahoa Church, the Church of the Kings in Honolulu, a plaque honors Queen Kaahumanu: "Although naturally proud and haughty, she labored earnestly to lead her people to Christ. She was a distinguished reformer of her nation . . . and a faithful comforter of the infant churches in these isles." Moments before Kaahumanu died, on June 5, 1832, Hiram Bingham gave her the first edition of the New Testament in the Hawaiian language, which had just come off the press. Her last words were from a Hawaiian hymn. The English translation is "Lo, here am I, O Jesus; grant me Thy gracious smile."[204]

---

[201]Roddy, "Amazing Queen," 5.

[202]Ibid.

[203]Fullard-Leo, "Woman Who Changed."

[204]Roddy, "Amazing Queen," 5.

August 21, 2011
P. T. Forsyth

Peter Taylor Forsyth, better known as P. T. Forsyth, is an important figure in Congregational history. He was born in Aberdeen, Scotland, in 1848, and he died in London in 1921. He served Congregational churches in England, but he also lectured in the United States. As a young man, he studied in Germany and was greatly influenced by the liberal theology of Albrecht Ritschl, casting a very critical eye on the authority of Scripture and on evangelical theology. However, in his later years, he began to see liberal theology as thin and lacking in intellectual and spiritual value.

In a time when major Congregational pastors and scholars were moving away from the thinking of the Puritans, Forsyth was one of those who moved back toward them. However, as Sydney Ahlstrom points out, Forsyth was "only belatedly discovered in the United States."[205] Alister McGrath, a great theologian of our time, quotes Forsyth with approval: "There is nothing we are told more often by those who would discard an evangelical faith than this—that we must now . . . return to the religion of Jesus. We are bidden to go back to practise Jesus' own personal religion, as distinct from the Gospel of Christ, from a gospel which calls him its faith's object, and not its subject. . . . But . . . as far back as we can go, we find only the belief and worship of a risen, redeeming, and glorified Christ, whom they could wholly trust but only very poorly imitate; and in his relation to God could not imitate at all."[206]

On decision-making in a Congregational church, Forsyth had this to say: "Majorities and minorities are not the calculus of the Spirit. . . . We must look for a power which is immune from a mere majority. We look to an electorate in no form, but to an Elector, His choice, His historic gift, and His Holy Spirit in His church, and no majority vote can guarantee the presence of His will."[207] On where the Church gets its authority, he said: "When any

---

[205] Ahlstrom, 936, note.

[206] Peter Taylor Forsyth, "On the Person of Christ," in *The Christian Theology Reader*, ed. Alister E. McGrath (Malden: Blackwell Publishing, 2001), 302.

[207] Forsyth, *The Principle of Authority* (Blackwood: New Creation Publications, 2004), 234 «http://www.newcreation.org.au/books/pdf/397_Principle_of_Authority.pdf» (accessed 29 Apr 2012).

community ceases to care whether it is a real Church of the apostolic Gospel, so long as it is for the hour rationally free, pious and social, that simply means that evangelical liberty, the release of the conscience from itself by God for God, has been lost in the assertive liberty of the atomic, unhistoric, natural man exercised on a religious matter. Such a body then means nothing for the Gospel anymore. To renounce the Word is, in principle, to dissolve the Church."[208]

On the kind of creative theology that he had admired in his youth, he wrote later: "There is a popular impression about both philosophy and theology that [they are] a scene in which each newcomer demolishes the work of his predecessor in order to put in its place some theory doomed in turn to the same fruitless fate. . . . If it were so with theology, we should not only be distressed for Humanity, but we should be skeptical about the Holy Spirit in the Church. It could be the Church of no Holy Spirit if those who translated its life into thought did not offer to posterity a spectacle higher than dragons that tore each other in the slime, or lions that bit and devoured one another."[209]

Forsyth's view of the pastor's position in a Congregational church is worth quoting: "The work of the ministry labours under one heavy disadvantage when we regard it as a profession and compare it with other professions. In these, experience brings facility, a sense of mastery in the subject, self-satisfaction, self-confidence; but in our subject the more we pursue it . . . the more . . . we . . . sense not only . . . our insufficiency, but . . . our unworthiness. . . . We have to handle the gospel. We have to lift up Christ—a Christ who is the death of natural self-confidence—a humiliating, even a crushing Christ; and we are not always alive to our uplifting and resurrection in Him. We have to handle a gospel that is a new rebuke to us every step we gain in intimacy with it. There is no real intimacy with the gospel which does not mean a new sense of God's holiness. . . . And there is no new sense of the holy God that does not arrest His name upon our unclean lips."[210]

---

[208]Ibid., 252.

[209]Forsyth, *The Work of Christ* (Blackwood: New Creation Publications, 1994), 175-176 « www.newcreation.org.au/books/pdf/277_WorkOfChrist.pdf» (accessed 29 Apr 2012).

[210]Forsyth, *The Soul of Prayer* (Blackwood: New Creation Publications, 1999), 71 « www.newcreation.org.au/books/pdf/331_SoulPrayer.pdf» (accessed 29 Apr 2012).

August 28, 2011
Henry Martyn Dexter

Henry Martyn Dexter was born in 1821 in Massachusetts and died in 1890. He was one of the most prominent Congregational pastors of his time. Not only was he a recognized expert on early Congregationalists like Robert Browne, but he was also in the forefront of efforts to organize Congregational churches on a national scale and to put out statements explaining what basic beliefs most Congregationalists held in common. Of course, in our tradition no one is forced to recite such creeds—although there have been many Congregational creeds over the centuries—our position has been that a creed is "a testimony, not a test."[211]

Dexter wrote many books explaining and defending the Congregational Way. In the nineteenth century, it was still not uncommon to give very long titles to books. One of his titles was *Congregationalism, What It Is, Whence It Is, How It Works, Why It Is Better Than Any Other Form of Church Government, and Its Consequent Demands.* He was also one of the editors of *The Congregationalist* magazine. As well, Dexter wrote and translated hymns. There is nothing by him in our hymnal, but in an old Methodist hymnal I found "Shepherd of Eager Youth," written by Clement of Alexandria in the late second century or early third century and translated by Henry Martyn Dexter.[212]

Some of you may be surprised to hear that, in some ways, Dexter was too conservative even for me. Not only did he oppose the ordination of women, for example, but he did not believe that women should even have the right to vote in congregational or associational meetings.[213] But Dexter loved the Congregational Way, and he had a very good understanding of what a Congregational church ought to be like. He never claimed that Baptists or Methodists or members of other denominations were not true Christians; he

---

[211]"Got Questions Ministries" «http://www.gotquestions.org/congregationalism.html» (accessed 29 Apr 2012).

[212]Carlton R. Young, ed., *The Book of Hymns* (Nashville: The United Methodist Publishing House, 1966), 86.

[213]Von Rohr, 294.

simply maintained that our system was the best way of organizing Christian churches.

In the book with the long title mentioned above, Dexter wrote, "Congregationalism is the democratic form of church order and government. It derives its name from the prominence which it gives to the *congregation* of Christian believers. It vests all ecclesiastical power (under Christ) in the associated brotherhood of each local church, as an independent body. At the same time it recognizes a fraternal and equal fellowship between these independent churches, which invests each with the right and duty of advice and reproof, and even of the public withdrawal of that fellowship in case the course pursued by another of the sisterhood should demand such action for the preservation of its own purity and consistency."[214]

In another book called *Handbook of Congregationalism*, Dexter distinguished between two opposing tendencies in Congregationalism, which he called Brownism (after Robert Browne) and Barrowism (after Henry Barrow, another early Congregationalist pastor). Brownism, in Dexter's view, and also in the view of many Congregational scholars in our time, was to be preferred. Barrowism put authority in the local church into the hands of presiding elders, whom the people of the church chose once and only once; after that, they never had any more authority over them. This, Dexter said, represented our ever-present temptation toward Presbyterianism. Brownism, Dexter believed, properly put all authority in the local church into the hands of the people, as long as they recognized the superior authority of Jesus and allowed themselves to be guided by the Holy Spirit.

In the same book, Dexter insisted that the Bible teaches Congregationalism: "There is, then, for there can be, but one conclusion. The system of church polity existing in the beginning . . . was essential Congregationalism. [It was based on] ecclesiastical democracy, in sharp, continual, and irreconcilable hostility with spiritual aristocracy or monarchy."[215] (p. 41).

---

[214]Henry M. Dexter, *Congregationalism, What It Is, Whence It Is, How It Works, Why It Is Better Than Any Other Form of Church Government, and Its Consequent Demands* (Boston: Nichols and Noyes, 1865), 1-2 «http://books.google.com» (accessed 29 Apr 2012).

[215]Dexter, *A Hand-book of Congregationalism* (Boston: Congregational Publishing Society, 1880), 41 « http://www.kobobooks.com/ebook/A-handbook-of-

Dexter is probably most famous for his well-known definition of Congregationalism as "an ellipse with two foci: local autonomy, and fellowship."[216]

Congregationalism/book-ZWoIayRr4kqyuLJF9XO0Mg/page1.html» (accessed 29 Apr 2012).

[216]Hartley, unpublished lecture notes, Congregational History and Polity Seminar, Boston, July 2011.

September 4, 2011
Washington Gladden

We have spent the last two sessions discussing two of the important conservative thinkers in nineteenth-century Congregationalism. Maybe it's time to provide some balance by mentioning one of the most prominent and most beloved of our nineteenth-century liberals: Washington Gladden.

Gladden was born in 1836. He served churches in New England at first. Sydney Ahlstrom points out that Gladden "was among the few that counseled moderation . . . after Lincoln's assassination. He pointed out that Booth got little or no applause in the South. But Gladden admitted that his words were very coldly received, affecting the course of the nation about as much 'as the chirping of the swallows on the telegraph pole affects the motion of the Twentieth Century Limited.' "[217]

But Gladden's influence was strongest when he served for more than thirty years at First Congregational Church in Columbus, Ohio, beginning in the 1880's. He was among those who questioned the authority of the Bible and who supported Darwinian evolution. According to James Sawyer, "He once urged his denomination to refuse a substantial donation from Standard Oil Company, calling it 'tainted money.' "[218] Norris Magnuson said that Gladden "has been called the father of the social gospel."[219]

The Social Gospel movement was most famously championed by Walter Rauschenbusch, a pastor in the German Baptist denomination. Just as Gladden was influenced by Horace Bushnell before him, so Rauschenbusch acknowledged his debt to Gladden. Rauschenbusch wrote in *A Theology for the Social Gospel*: "The social gospel is the old message of salvation, but enlarged and intensified. The individualistic gospel has taught us to see the sinfulness of every human heart and has inspired us with faith in the willingness and power of God to save every soul that comes to him. But it has not given us an adequate understanding of the sinfulness of the social order

---

[217]Ahlstrom, 688, note.

[218]Sawyer, 33.

[219]Norris A. Magnuson, "Social Gospel, The," in Elwell, 1028.

and its share in the sins of all individuals within it."[220]   Gladden and Rauschenbusch died in the same year, 1918.

George Fry, writing in *The Congregationalist* in March 1975, told about Gladden's sense of humor. A businessman was introduced to Gladden as "Dr. Gladden" and naturally assumed that he was a physician. "Sir, where do you practice?" he asked. Gladden chuckled and answered, "Oh, I don't practice, I just preach."[221] However, Fry reports, not everyone was charmed by Gladden: Billy Sunday said these words, apparently about Gladden and his followers: "They're a bad lot, Lord Jesus, a bad lot. Let me give you a tip, Lord Jesus. If you go after those fellows, you'd better put on your rubber gloves."[222]

Other famous people were more sympathetic. Theodore Roosevelt, then the police commissioner of New York City, spoke from Gladden's pulpit. City planners were influenced by Gladden's plans for urban renewal. Gladden himself entered politics, being elected to the Columbus City Council for a two-year term. Although he never formally became a socialist, Gladden did advocate public ownership of utilities and worker management of factories.

Gladden was dismayed at the use of evolutionary theory by the "Social Darwinists": "What men call 'natural law,' by which they mean the law of greed and strife . . . is not a natural law; it is unnatural; it is a crime against nature; the law of brotherhood is the only natural law. The law of nature is the law of sympathy, of fellowship, of mutual help and service."[223]

Our National Association has a Washington Gladden Society, dedicated to "applying the insights of the Social Gospel Movement to the important, controversial ethical and theological issues of our own times. ..."[224]

---

[220]Walter Rauschenbusch, *A Theology for the Social Gospel* (New York: The Macmillan Company, 1917), 5.

[221]C. George Fry, "Washington Gladden: Congregationalist," *The Congregationalist*, March 1975, 10, in Larson.

[222]Ibid., 12.

[223]Ibid.

[224]"Washington Gladden Society" «http://washingtongladdensociety.org/about.html» (accessed 29 Apr 2012).

I am most grateful to Washington Gladden for writing one of my very favorite hymns: "O Master, Let Me Walk with Thee."[225]

---

[225]Kelly Dobbs Mickus, ed., *Hymns for a Pilgrim People* (Oak Creek: Congregational Press, 2007), 436.

September 11, 2011
D. L. Moody

Dwight Lyman Moody was born in 1837 in Northfield, Massachusetts. The story is told that a neighbor stuck his head through the open window of the one-room schoolhouse where Dwight and his five brothers were. "You got any of Ed Moody's kids here?" the neighbor asked the schoolteacher. "Well, you'd better send them home. Their father just died."[226] In later years, Dwight Moody would say: "The first thing I remember was the death of my father. It was a beautiful day in June when he fell suddenly dead. The shock made such an impression on me, young as I was, that I shall never forget it."[227]

With eight children to feed, Dwight's mother had to send some of her children off to workhouses. Dwight was fed enough to eat, but it was porridge and milk, every day, three times a day. Mrs. Moody still insisted that all her children attend the Unitarian church with her every Sunday. Dwight left Northfield for Boston at age seventeen.

Dwight's uncle gave him a job in his Boston shoe store, with the condition that Dwight attend a Congregational church. After about a year, Edward Kimball, Dwight's Sunday School teacher, led him to the Lord. Dwight moved to Chicago in 1856, working as a successful and well-known shoe salesman. There, he established a church school for children in the slums in 1858. A non-combatant during the Civil War, Dwight served with the YMCA, accompanying the Union troops throughout the war. After the war, he became the president of the YMCA in Chicago. He was also influential in reviving the Sunday School Union.

Peter Marshall, Jr., reports, "In Chicago, a shoe salesman who had moved there from Boston was astonished when the merchant he was calling on looked at his watch and said he had to go to a prayer meeting. Already converted . . . the shoe salesman went with him. . . . Soon the salesman wrote home . . . 'I go to meeting every night. Oh, how I enjoy it! It seems as if God

---

[226]Harry J. Albus, "The Boy from Northfield," in *Of People*, ed. Jan Anderson (Pensacola: A Beka Books, 2008), 35.

[227]M. Laird Simons, "Dwight Lyman Moody," *Wholesome Words: Christian Biography Resources* «www.wholesomewords.org/biography/biomoody.html» (accessed 4 September 2011).

were here Himself. O Mother, pray . . . that this work may go on till every knee is bowed!' . . . Dwight L. Moody would turn in his shoe sample kit and go into full-time evangelism."[228]

Beginning in about 1870, Moody joined the long line of evangelistic preachers that stretches from the Great Awakening down to Billy Graham and Luis Palau in our day. Moody and his music leader, Ira Sankey, preached to two and a half million people in Great Britain and to many millions more in the United States. At the 1889 meeting of the National Council of Congregational Churches, Moody was commended as "the most successful evangelist of our time."[229] Moody preached to the poor with great results, but he also appealed strongly to the middle class because of his solid business background. *Webster's Guide to American History* tells us, "The substance of his preaching was a simple, conservative, personal Christianity sharply in contrast with the Social Gospel movement of the same period."[230] However, Justo González writes, "He was convinced that the conversion of the masses would lead to better living conditions in the cities, and therefore he had little to say regarding the conditions and structures that led to so much human misery."[231] Sydney Ahlstrom describes Moody's style: "Holding aloft his Bible, he assured his hearers that eternal life was theirs for the asking, that they had only to 'come forward and t-a-k-e, TAKE!' This done, his follow-up instruction was short and to the point: 'Join some church at once.' "[232]

Moody's evangelistic headquarters was in his hometown of Northfield. There, he established Northfield Seminary for girls in 1879 and Mount Hermon School for boys in 1881. In 1889, Moody founded the Chicago Bible Institute, which continues today as the Moody Bible Institute. The Moody Bible Institute consists of an undergraduate Bible college with branches in several different cities, as well as a seminary, the Mission Aviation Fellowship, a publishing house, and a radio network with programs

---

[228]Marshall and Manuel, *Trumpet*, 427.

[229]Von Rohr, 330-331.

[230]Van Doren and McHenry, 1132.

[231]González, vol. 2, p. 254.

[232]Ahlstrom, 745.

on stations all over the United States. In addition, the Institute produces a daily devotional called *Today in the Word.*

September 18, 2011
Rev. Antoinette Brown

Antoinette Brown was the first woman ever to be ordained to Christian ministry.[233] She was born in 1825. When she was five years old, her father, Joseph Brown, became a Christian at one of Charles Finney's revivals, and Antoinette herself became a believer and joined a Congregational church four years later. She entered Oberlin College in 1845. At Oberlin, she met the famous feminist and abolitionist Lucy Stone, and they became lifelong friends. During school vacations, she taught school and studied Hebrew and Greek. After graduating in 1848, she began studying for the ministry. Her family did not support this ambition. Her parents disapproved, and so did her brother William, who was a pastor.

When Antoinette wrote a paper reinterpreting Paul's statement that apparently forbade women from speaking in church, it was printed in the *Oberlin Quarterly Review.* However, the school officials did their best to discourage her. They told her that she might reasonably plan to become a missionary, but not a pastor.[234] She was ostracized from the society of her all-male classmates, and her professors mostly ignored her. Antoinette completed her studies at Oberlin in 1850, but granting a theological degree to a woman was seen as inappropriate, and she was not given the degree and not allowed to participate in the commencement ceremony.

Charles Finney encouraged Antoinette to speak publicly, and she gave public lectures for three years after finishing her studies. She also wrote for Frederick Douglass's newspaper, the *North Star*, and she spoke at the National Women's Rights Convention in 1850. Unlike many other "progressive" thinkers of her time, Antoinette opposed the evolutionary theory advanced by Charles Darwin and Herbert Spencer. Unlike many other crusaders for women's rights, she was adamantly opposed to divorce.

Finally, in 1853, Antoinette was called to First Congregational Church of Butler and Savannah in Wayne County, New York, for an annual salary of three hundred dollars. (Even though the dollar was worth much more in those days, this was still a very small amount of money.) Because the church

---

[233]Von Rohr, 274.

[234]W. T. Keefe, "Women in the Pastoral Ministry," *The Congregationalist*, October 1982, 6, in Larson.

building was too small and a large crowd wanted to attend, Antoinette was ordained on September 15, 1853, in a Baptist church building. A Methodist minister, Rev. Luther Lee, who had previously been opposed to ordaining women, preached her ordination sermon, and his text was Galatians 3:28 ("There is neither Jew nor Greek, bond nor free, male nor female, for you are all one in Christ Jesus").

Antoinette's ministry in New York was short-lived. She was much more liberal in her theology than most of her church members were. She resigned her pastorate in July 1854. She moved to New York City and did social work. She wrote articles on social issues for Horace Greeley's *New York Tribune*. In 1856, she married Samuel Blackwell, moved to New Jersey, and accepted the occasional invitation to preach in various liberal churches.[235] Antoinette and Samuel had seven children, but two died in infancy.

Antoinette returned to public life eventually, again attending the National Women's Rights Convention in 1860 and being one of the founders of the American Woman Suffrage Association in 1869. (Oberlin College, by the way, finally thought better of its refusal of a degree to Antoinette Brown Blackwell, and in 1878 she was awarded the master of arts. Thirty years after that, Oberlin would give her the honorary degree of doctor of divinity.) Antoinette returned to the ministry in 1878, but this time as a Unitarian minister. She founded All Souls Unitarian Church in Elizabeth, New Jersey, and she served as that church's pastor for forty-three years, until her death. Antoinette Brown Blackwell lived long enough finally to be able to vote. In 1920, she reported that she had voted for Warren G. Harding for President. She died the following year, at age ninety-six.

---

[235]Hartley, lecture notes.

September 25, 2011
Charles M. Sheldon

In the 1990's, a fad swept through the world of Christian young people. A certain slogan appeared on T-shirts, on jewelry, and on many other items of merchandise that were sold in Christian bookstores. Interestingly enough, this brand-new fad was really a hundred years old, being based on a novel written by a Congregational pastor in 1896.

Charles M. Sheldon was one of the leaders of the Social Gospel movement, sometimes called Christian Socialism. Charles Sheldon was born February 26, 1857, in Wellsville, New York. He was the son of a minister, and as a child he lived in a log cabin in the Dakota Territory for a few years. In 1889, he became pastor of a new church, Central Congregational Church in Topeka, Kansas.

Sheldon had great sympathy for poor people. He spent a lot of time ministering to the black people in the Topeka neighborhood called Tennesseetown.[236] During the depression of the 1890's, Sheldon wanted to know how the unemployed felt. He put on some old clothes and applied for a job at every business in Topeka. He was turned down every single time. Sheldon founded an organization called the Village Improvement Society, which (among other things) found jobs for many unemployed people.

Even though he was a tremendously popular preacher, Sheldon worked for many years at his church without ever asking for a raise in his salary. During this time he wrote thirty books, as well as many articles, editorials, and poems. For a time, while still serving as pastor of Central Church, he was also the editor of one of Topeka's major newspapers, the *Daily Capital*.

In those days, most American churches still had Sunday-night services in addition to their Sunday-morning worship. However, Sunday-night attendance at Sheldon's church was not very high. In order to increase attendance, he started telling very entertaining and very popular story sermons. In 1896, he began a series, essentially a novel with each sermon a different chapter, titled "In His Steps." Eventually, this became a book, after it was published in installments in a Congregational magazine called the *Chicago Advance*. However, the magazine neglected to copyright the story,

---

[236]Butman, "Following in His Steps," *The Congregationalist*, June 1984, 18, in Larson.

and over sixty-six publishers worldwide put out editions without paying Sheldon anything. There were translations into twenty-one languages, even including Arabic. (Oddly and somewhat ironically, the Union of Soviet Socialist Republics would later ban the Russian version of this novel written by a Christian Socialist.) The book version of *In His Steps* became a huge best-seller not only in the United States but around the world.

In His Steps is the story of Rev. Henry Maxwell, a fictitious pastor of a prosperous church, not unlike Charles Sheldon. While he was working on his sermon one Friday night, a shabby man came to his door. Pastor Maxwell was busy, so he turned the man away. But his conscience bothered him as he watched the poor, dejected tramp walk away with his head down and his hands in his pockets. On Sunday morning, he had a surprise. At the end of the service, the very same man walked up the aisle and stood in front of the pulpit. The man began to speak: "I'm not an ordinary tramp, though I don't know of any teaching of Jesus that makes one kind of a tramp less worth saving than another. Do you? . . . I lost my job ten months ago. . . . Of course, I understand you can't all go out of your way to hunt up jobs for other people like me. I'm not asking you to; but what I feel puzzled about is, what is meant by following Jesus. . . . Do you mean that you are suffering and denying yourselves and trying to save lost, suffering humanity just as I understand Jesus did? What do you mean by it?"[237] The man fainted after his speech, and a few days later he was dead, leaving behind a little girl, the child of the man and his late wife.

The following Sunday, Maxwell preached, "I want volunteers from First Church who will pledge themselves, earnestly and honestly for an entire year, not to do anything without first asking the question, 'What would Jesus do?' "[238]

---

[237]Charles Sheldon, *In His Steps* (New York: Grosset & Dunlap, 1935), 8-9.

[238]Ibid., 15.

October 9, 2011
Burial Hill and Oberlin

Dr. Harry R. Butman reports, "The westward expansion of Congregationalism after the Albany Convention of 1852 demonstrated the need for a national body of Congregational Churches. Accordingly, after much consultation, a provisional National Council assembled in Boston, June 14, 1865.

"The Council addressed two major questions—what do American Congregationalists believe; and, what is their mode of government? The debate on the point of a national confession of faith was long and sometimes acrimonious, and it was still unsettled when the council adjourned to a special session in Plymouth, on Burial Hill where Pilgrim dust reposed. Rev. Alonzo Quint wrote [what became known as 'The Burial Hill Declaration of Faith']. In a dramatic historical setting, the 'Declaration' was approved with two dissenting votes."[239]

Beginning with a very eloquent historical prologue which is too long to quote in full, the Declaration then says, in part, "It was the faith of our fathers that gave us this free land in which we dwell. It is by this faith only that we can transmit to our children a free and happy, because a Christian, commonwealth. . . .

"Recognizing the unity of the Church of Christ in all the world, and knowing that we are but one branch of Christ's people, while adhering to our peculiar faith and order, we extend to all believers the hand of Christian fellowship upon the basis of those great fundamental truths in which all Christians should agree. . . ."[240]

Another important document produced by the Council was the "Statement of the Principles of Congregational Polity." Butman says that it "was the work of a committee of influential pastors, laymen, and professors. It affirmed the autonomy of the local Church [and] the communion . . . of the Churches, and [it] limited the powers of ministers."[241]

---

[239]Butman, *Symbols*, 11.

[240]Walker, 563.

[241]Butman, *Symbols*, 11.

Partly as a result of the success of the 1865 meeting, a permanent National Council of Congregational Churches was formed in November 1871 at Oberlin, Ohio. "The Oberlin Declaration" says (again quoting only parts of it), "The Congregational churches of the United States, by elders and messengers assembled, do now associate themselves in National Council:

"To express and foster their substantial unity in doctrine, polity, and work. . . .

"They agree in belief that the Holy Scriptures are the sufficient and only infallible rule of religious faith and practice; their interpretation thereof being in substantial accordance with the great doctrines of the Christian faith, commonly called Evangelical, held in our churches from the early times. . . .

"They agree in belief that the right of government resides in local churches, or congregations of believers, who are responsible directly to the Lord Jesus Christ, the One Head of the Church universal and of all particular churches; but that all churches . . . have mutual duties subsisting in the obligations of fellowship.

"The churches, therefore, while establishing this National Council for the furtherance of the common interests and work of all the churches, do maintain the scriptural and inalienable right of each church to self-government and administration; and this National Council shall never exercise legislative or judicial authority, nor consent to act as a council of reference."[242]

That last paragraph, by the way, would become very important in the next century, as it clearly supports the position of our current National Council that the formation of the United Church of Christ was completely inappropriate and even illegal.

Critics have pointed out that there is no mention of the concept of covenant in either the Burial Hill Declaration or the Oberlin Declaration. However, John von Rohr writes, "Designed to be ecumenical in nature . . . the [Burial Hill Declaration], however, did uphold a Trinitarian view of God, thereby ruling out the Unitarian view. . . ."[243]

---

[242]Walker, 573.

[243]Von Rohr, 282.

October 23, 2011
The Commission Creed

As we learned from the start, when we looked at the early years of Congregationalism, our movement—which we are repeatedly told has no creeds—has produced a large number of creeds over the years. Last time, we looked at the Burial Hill Declaration of Faith. This week, we are taking a glance at the Commission Creed of 1883. It is called the Commission Creed because it was produced by a commission created by the National Council of Congregational Churches in 1880. Actually, and somewhat humorously, the commission was created indirectly by the Council, who appointed "a committee of seven," who selected the twenty-five members of the commission, including Henry Martyn Dexter.[244]

One interesting thing about this document is that there is absolutely no pretense here that Congregationalists have no creeds. The National Council directed the commission to prepare "in the form of a Creed or Catechism, or both . . . a simple, clear, and comprehensive exposition of the truths of the Glorious Gospel of the Blessed God, for the instruction and edification of our churches."[245]

Now, if you read some of the literature prepared by our Association in the present day, you might get the impression that Congregationalists are encouraged to believe just any old thing they want, or even to believe nothing at all if they so choose. But the intent of this document seems to be the opposite: it is communicating that Congregationalists are in fact evangelical Christians who believe the truths taught in the Bible and who are completely orthodox in their beliefs. There is very little in its twelve articles that is explicitly Congregational.

Article I is a very clear statement that we believe in the Trinity, and it defines the Trinity in a shortened version of the language of the Nicene Creed. Article II stresses that we believe both in God's undefeatable plan and in human free will and responsibility. Article III resembles the Westminster Confession, in teaching that we are made in God's image for the purpose of knowing Him and enjoying Him forever. Article IV states that God wants all human beings to be saved, and that He has provided both general revelation

---

[244]Walker, 579.

[245]Schaff, vol. 3, pp. 913-914.

through His creation and special revelation through His Holy Word. Article V states specifically that the Scriptures were written by men under the inspiration of the Holy Spirit to reveal God to humankind. Article VI tells about Jesus' holy life and undeserved death and how He accomplished our salvation at the cross. Article VII affirms that Jesus has ascended into heaven where He intercedes for us and whence He has sent the Holy Spirit to us. Article VIII reminds us that the Holy Spirit is continuing to sanctify us "and that the believer's hope of continuance in such a life is in the preserving grace of God." Article IX emphasizes that Christ is our King and that we have access to Him without any mediator between us and Him. Article XI discusses the meeting together of believers on the Lord's Day and the administration of the only two sacraments, baptism and the Lord's Supper. Article XII witnesses to the truth that Jesus will come in final judgment, resurrecting the dead to either everlasting punishment or everlasting life.

You might notice that I did not mention Article X. That is the only one of the twelve that is truly Congregational in emphasis. Although it does not use the word "covenant," it does communicate our belief in the nature of the local church: "We believe that the Church of Christ, invisible and spiritual, comprises all true believers, whose duty it is to associate themselves in churches, for the maintenance of worship, for the promotion of spiritual growth and fellowship, and for the conversion of man; that these churches, under the guidance of the Holy Scriptures and in fellowship with one another, may determine—each for itself—their organization, statements of belief, and forms of worship; may appoint and set apart their own ministers; and should cooperate in the work which Christ has committed to them for the furtherance of the gospel throughout the world."[246]

---

[246]Walker, 580-582.

November 6, 2011
The Kansas City Statement

We don't want to discuss our Congregational creeds every single week, but it would be irresponsible to ignore the Kansas City Statement of 1913. Different historians have different interpretations of what the Kansas City Statement, or the Kansas City Creed, was all about. John von Rohr, for example, sees it as a triumph of theological liberalism: "The older pattern of tracing a personal pilgrimage from sin to salvation was abandoned. . . . The statement instead, in the mood of the social gospel, mainly emphasized the churches' striving to know God's will . . . and to labor for justice, peace, and human 'brotherhood.' It then ended with its vision and faith for the future, expressed as the transformation of the world into the Kingdom of God. . . . There was no mention of evolution, but the tone and the optimism were of the New Theology. Washington Gladden called it a 'noble Confession of Faith' and declared, 'We can write that on our banner and go forth . . . to conquer.'"[247]

Williston Walker's *Creeds and Platforms of Congregationalism* sees the document as somewhat of a retreat from the Congregational ideal of the autonomous local church: "Several recent developments made it increasingly evident that the denomination needed a national structure with real, and not merely advisory, authority. . . . As a consequence, two special committees were authorized at the council meeting of 1907 to [discuss] the future of the denomination. A Committee of Fifteen, reporting in Boston three years later, reached no firm conclusions; but a Committee on Polity [submitted] several far-reaching resolutions. These affirmed the strengthening of state conferences and associations; formally enlarged the moderator's function to include service between national meetings; and reshaped the office of secretary into one of active leadership. . . . The Committee on Polity recommended that another group be appointed to consider further [issues of denominational structure]. Thus was the Commission of Nineteen appointed. ... In the prefatory statement to its report at the National Council in Kansas City, Missouri, in October 1913, the chair and secretary of the group [reported that the] votes leading to the final adoption of the report . . . were 'notable alike for what they manifested of individual loyalty to conscience and a wonderful and vital unity that binds us together as a denomination.' That

---

[247]Von Rohr, 356.

sense of unity . . . pointed toward a new era for Congregationalism as a corporate body, as a *church*, not only as a loose aggregate of church*es*."[248]

Those who wrote the document might have disagreed with both Von Rohr's and Walker's interpretations. Like earlier statements, the Kansas City Statement was described by one of its authors, Rev. Dr. William E. Barton, as "not a series of creedal articles, but . . . an inclusive statement of the essential things most surely believed by Christians."[249]

However, the document is not only a broadly evangelical statement of faith, but it also clearly supports a congregational polity. Here is the section on church government: "We believe in the freedom and responsibility of the individual soul, and the right of private judgment. We hold to the autonomy of the local church and its independence of all ecclesiastical control. We cherish the fellowship of the churches, united in district, state, and national bodies, for counsel and cooperation in matters of common concern."[250]

It is not necessary to quote the Kansas City Creed at length, for the simple reason that the language of our own Church of the Oaks Covenant and Statement of Faith is almost word-for-word from the Kansas City Statement. But let's close with the beginning few words of the Creed, some very inspiring language that is not copied in our own Bylaws: "We believe in God the Father, infinite in wisdom, goodness and love, and in Jesus Christ, His Son, our Lord and Savior, Who for us and for our salvation lived and died and rose again and liveth evermore, and in the Holy Spirit, Who taketh of the things of Christ and revealeth them to us, renewing, comforting, and inspiring the souls of men."[251]

---

[248]Walker, 595-597.

[249]Schaff, vol. 3, p. 915.

[250]Walker, 600.

[251]Ibid., 599.

November 13, 2011
Birth of the NACCC

October 25 has come and gone this year, but we should have all told each other "Happy birthday!" on that date. Why? Because on October 25, 1956, the National Association of Congregational Christian Churches was formed. This was an act of great courage and heroism and faith: in the face of the wholesale abandonment of the Congregational Way by most of America's Congregational churches, a little remnant decided to act to preserve that Way.

It is hard to pinpoint exactly when certain historical developments had their beginning, but we could argue that it was those nineteenth-century creeds, and the Kansas City Statement of 1913, that caused the General Council of Congregational Christian Churches to begin seeing itself as a denomination, with authority over all the local Congregational churches. Certainly, those creeds did advocate a more coherent organization binding us all together, but it would be a stretch to see them as pushing for an authoritarian hierarchy.

In the 1940's, many Congregational voices were calling for a merger between the Evangelical and Reformed Church and the Congregational Christian Churches (which would eventually take effect, in 1957, forming the United Church of Christ). Many leaders in the General Council, seeing the Council as a governing body, assumed that it had the right to make this merger happen simply by voting to unite with the other group. However, those who opposed the merger pointed out that the General Council had no authority over local churches; that it could not merge with any denomination because it was not, in fact, "the Congregational denomination," but merely the agent of the local churches; and that it would be inappropriate for us to merge with the Evangelical and Reformed Church, anyway, because it was not an association of free churches but in fact was organized like the Presbyterian denomination.

In 1950, the General Council appointed a Committee on Free Church Unity and Polity. That committee issued a report in 1954 that was accepted by the General Council. The report forcefully affirmed our commitment to Congregational principles. Here are a few quotations from that report: "Congregationalism believes that the church is both local and universal. While the one aspect is not to be stressed at the expense of the other, Congregationalism has always been sensitively aware of the danger of losing sight of the completeness of the local church, which within itself compasses both the local and the universal. . . . We have insisted on the autonomy of the local church [based on] a seeking of and a following of the guidance of the

Holy Spirit by the people of this gathered church."[252] "The General Council of the Congregational Christian Churches of the United States is a voluntary organization of the Congregational Christian churches."[253] "The General Council is not a legislative body with ecclesiastical authority over the churches. . . . No coercion or threat of coercion of any type may be used to compel a local church to comply with the wishes of General Council leaders...."[254]

Foreseeing that the General Council would ignore these statements, a few Congregational leaders met in Detroit in 1955. Written a year later, the preamble to our Articles of Association ends with this paragraph: "Therefore we, the Churches by our delegates here assembled in Wauwatosa, Wisconsin this 25th day of October, 1956, do covenant in this National Association of Congregational Christian Churches to walk together in the ways which God anciently revealed to our fathers, and in such further ways as He may yet reveal to us. . . . Amen."[255]

Writing about all this a few decades later, Harry Butman said, "This bold and necessary action by the faithful minority made certain that the historic Congregational idea of the autonomy of the local Church under the Headship of Christ, and the fellowship of the Churches, would not sink into ecclesiastical oblivion in our time, nor the hallowed name of Congregationalism cease to be spoken. We of the National Association are the custodians of the Pilgrim Heritage. Before us lies the good work of the continuation and extension of our Way."[256]

---

[252]Steven A. Peay and Lloyd M. Hall, Jr., eds., *The 1954 Polity and Unity Report* (Oak Creek: Congregational Press, 2001), 16-17.

[253]Ibid., 28.

[254]Ibid., 30.

[255]Butman, *Symbols*, 13.

[256]Ibid., 13-14.

November 20, 2011
The Chislehurst Thanksgiving

Last week, we talked about how most of the Congregational churches in the United States really abandoned the Congregational Way by becoming part of the United Church of Christ. This kind of merger, in which Congregational churches lost their identity, occurred in other countries as well: in England, in Canada, and in Australia, for example.

This was a huge step backward for the Congregational movement, which had seen great promise ahead at the end of the nineteenth century. The International Congregational Council was formed in 1891 in London, with representatives from all over the world. Weakened by the mergers that kept absorbing the Congregational churches in so many nations, the International Congregational Council itself finally was absorbed into a Presbyterian alliance in 1970.

In 1975, the International Congregational Fellowship was formed in Chislehurst, Kent, England. This was to be an organization representing the faithful remnant of non-merging Congregational churches in all countries. For that occasion, our own Harry R. Butman wrote a document called "The Chislehurst Thanksgiving." Here are some words from that document.

"From the far places of the world, from the east and from the west, we have walked the Congregational Way to this meeting under the favor of Almighty God and by the leading of the Holy Spirit, to reaffirm our allegiance to Christ as faithful coworkers with Him according to the Word of God, and in reliance on His sure promise that He is with us in our gathering.

"Although stress and strain and schism across the years have brought us to this place and day, we come not in sadness or in rancor, but with a strong and sober joy that we are accounted worthy to witness to the Way our fathers walked, and which, through the mercy of God, the Headship of Christ, and the communion of the Spirit, our children may travel after us in the generations to come. . . .

"We would not boldly presume to say that our declarations are binding upon the Churches, or upon the conscience of any Christian. . . . These are but some of the things centrally confessed by us in this hour of expectation, and they are said out of grateful hearts.

"We believe that the controlling truth of the Congregational Way is that Jesus is Lord: Great Head of His Church, both in its dear and local gatherings and in the awesome and eternal sweep of the Church Universal. Though we extol and defend the wholeness and completeness of each gathered local Church as our distinctive and cherished witness, we do not narrowly deny the validity of other Church orders, nor esteem them to be ways of darkness. 'The lamps are many; the Light is One.'

"We believe that independent local Congregational Churches should be joined in Fellowship—a free relation of affection. Ours is a brotherhood, a *koinonia*, a sharing which reaches out beyond those known and seen in a sense of mission to those whom 'having not seen, we love' in the bonds of Christ.

"Therefore we depart with thanksgiving from this place to which we came in quest and concern, rejoicing that God, by His power, and the prompting of the Spirit, has brought us to this fresh experience of Christ, and is sending us forth . . . to be steadfast witnesses to His Kingdom and His Church in all the world. In gratitude and testimony on this 13th day of May, 1975, we hereby set our hands, looking forward in hope to continuing our work and witness as the International Congregational Fellowship. In the name of God. *Amen.*"[257]

The International Congregational Fellowship, publisher of the *International Congregational Journal*, is still thriving today. Here are a couple of quotes from its Website: "Each church is governed by its members under the headship of Jesus Christ, respecting the authority of scripture and seeking to be led by the Holy Spirit. Our ministers or pastors, though usually well trained, do not act as priests or exercise authority over the congregation."[258]

---

[257]Butman, *Symbols*, 14-15.

[258]"International Congregational Fellowship" «http://www.intercong.org/about-us/history/» (accessed 29 Apr 2012).

December 4, 2011
Harry Butman

During this series of Congregational Minutes, I have often referred to, or quoted from, Dr. Harry R. Butman. Dr. Butman was one of the courageous founders of our National Association, and he was one of our most influential pastors, one of the editors of *The Congregationalist* magazine, one of the moderators of our annual meetings, one of the chairmen of our Executive Committee, and one of the major historians of our movement. He was born in Beverly, Massachusetts, and he died in Acton, California, on July 29, 2005, at the age of 101. He graduated from Bangor Theological Seminary in 1928 and was awarded the honorary degree of doctor of divinity by Piedmont College in 1958.

Dr. Butman was the author of many books. Let me quote from the brief biography on the back cover of one of those books, *The Lord's Free People*: "Dr. Harry R. Butman is a New Englander whose ancestral roots are deep in the Pilgrim earth. . . . As a minister his first three pastorates were within forty miles of Plymouth Rock. When he came to Los Angeles in 1953 to become the pastor of the Congregational Church of the Messiah, he brought earth from the yard of the ancient Church at Dedham to mingle with the adobe of a California hilltop as a token of his love for the Puritan way of life."[259]

Harry Butman was a clear thinker and an eloquent writer. In *The Congregationalist* for February 1968, he wrote an editorial called "The Car and the Pill," discussing what many have called "the sexual revolution." He mentioned the car because, he said, it "could be used as a bedroom on wheels." He went on to say, "I fear the avant-garde ideas of those clergymen of the new morality (which is neither new nor moral) who would throw aside all sexual restraint. A girl recently asked such a minister about the problem of premarital relations. 'What problem?' he countered. 'You no longer need fear disease or pregnancy. What's your problem?' There is a terrifying cheerfulness of ignorance about such an answer. Anyone who supposes that sex is merely a transient physical matter—blithely to bed and blithely to part in the *Playboy* manner—is utterly unaware of the nature of personality. Though the body go scatheless, there can be psychic traumas, scars on the

---

[259]Butman, *Lord's Free People*, back cover.

soul. Whoever thinks sex is a matter of flesh alone shares Freud's folly that man has no spiritual component."[260]

But my favorite article by Butman is from the February 1992 edition of our magazine, part of a series of articles about the right to bear arms: "On a blisteringly hot day . . . I sought for shade in the ghost town of Garlock. . . . As I sat there eating my lunch of a sandwich and a soft drink, a black car came drifting up. . . . The driver was a small, heavily-bearded man; three others were with him; they stared at me.

"The car went up the road a few hundred yards, turned, and came slowly back. It passed me a few yards away, and there was that in the eyes of the driver that sent me to the trunk of my car where I kept a Ruger .22 single six with a magnum cylinder. As I expected, the car turned north again, and as it rolled by I ostentatiously pumped shells into the piece. . . .

"The car did stop, not more than ten feet away. We stared in silence. ... To this day my conscience gives me trouble about my total lack of emotion. . . . I cannot understand my cold intellectual decision to kill this enemy if he opened his car door to come at me. . . .

"The confrontation ended abruptly when the driver broke the lock of staring, gunned his motor, and roared off to the south. . . . Shortly after . . . the old custodian of Holland Mine . . . told me that he was uneasy about a band of hippies camping on Goler Heights. The leader's name was Manson. . . .

"If I had shot Charlie Manson . . . pregnant murdered Sharon Tate's baby could now be a young adult. If I hadn't had a gun, I might well have been dead these twenty-three years, with a lot of fun missed, a fair amount of work for our Way undone, and this article unwritten."[261]

---

[260]Butman, "The Car and the Pill," *The Congregationalist*, February 1968, in Larson.

[261]Butman, "I Almost Shot Charles Manson," *The Congregationalist*, February 1992, 13-15, in Larson.

December 11, 2011
Arthur Rouner, Jr.

Last week we talked about Harry Butman, who was in the first generation of leaders of our National Association. Today, we will look at Arthur Rouner, Jr., a member of the second generation. His father, Arthur Rouner, Sr., could arguably be called *the* founder of the NACCC, since he was the one who filed the lawsuit in the state of New York in 1949 to stop the merger that would sink most Congregational churches into a non-Congregational organization.

Arthur Rouner, Jr., was ordained in his father's church. He earned a master's degree from Harvard and a doctorate from Union Theological Seminary, and he served as a Congregational pastor for over forty years. His longest tenure was at Colonial Church of Edina, Minnesota. He received several honors from community organizations during those years, and he became one of the most influential ministers in our Association.

After stepping down from his pastorate, Dr. Rouner founded the Pilgrim Center for Reconciliation in 1993. This is a ministry that is "committed to the work of healing and reconciliation in the aftermath of genocide, war, and debilitating conflict,"[262] according to one Website. The organization focuses on Africa, in such countries as Rwanda, Burundi, Congo, Kenya, Uganda, South Sudan, and Tanzania. But the ministry has also done work in India, and at home on American Indian reservations.

Dr. Rouner has written several books. One of the more recent is called *The Devilish Dialogues* (2003), a work that is something like C. S. Lewis's *The Screwtape Letters*. But his most famous work is no doubt his very first book, *The Congregational Way of Life*, published in 1960. (Several years ago, a group of us in this church spent several months studying that book, to our great profit.)

When asked how the book came to be, Dr. Rouner replied, "Well, I tried to preach about Congregationalism to my first little church . . . [and] the series of sermons was called 'The Congregational Way.' . . . Henry David Gray put up $100 as a little prize to have somebody write a book about the Congregational Way, based on the Savoy Platform. . . . So I took that as the

---

[262]"Pilgrim Center for Reconciliation" «http://www.razoo.com/story/Pilgrim-Center-For-Reconciliation» (accessed 29 Apr 2012).

basis for the book and then used what I could from these sermons. . . . [My father] stumbled onto Prentice Hall, who were publishing a series of books called the 'Way of Life' series—and there was *The Presbyterian Way of Life*, and *The Episcopal Way of Life*, and they were all written by famous people who were leaders in those denominations. And they didn't have one on the Congregational Way of Life . . . and they gave me an editor, we worked on it, and so it came to be. And I got the prize . . . and $100 didn't go very far, but—you know, it was a stimulus. . . ."[263]

Some of the important themes of that book are these: we are a covenant people; we live in freedom that is "bound by love";[264] we proclaim with the Church of all ages that Jesus is Lord; we are "the gathered church,"[265] gathered together by Jesus Himself; we are a people of the Word, taking the Bible very seriously as our authority; our pastors ideally are raised up from among our congregations; we are a people of the Holy Spirit, having been the original "Pentecostal" church centuries before the modern Pentecostal movement began; and our form of church government allows us to claim ecumenical fellowship with all true churches of every denomination.

In 1998, Dr. Rouner wrote an article called "Congregational Freedom," in which he decried the radical individualism that had come to dominate our churches. Looking back at our beginnings, he said, "The gift to the Church which those young people of independent England ... discovered and received was *the Spirit*, God's free, uncontrolled, moving, life-giving *Holy Spirit*. Congregationalism—to our surprise—was born as a Holy Spirit movement, living within a congregational autonomy that the Spirit made possible. . . . [The twenty-first] century must be the century of healing, of unity, of lives of love. . . . What a vision for us to embrace together!"[266]

---

[263] John Carson, "The Congregational Way of Life," *The Congregationalist*, September 2010, 21.

[264] Rouner, *Congregational Way*, 59.

[265] Ibid., 104.

[266] Rouner, "Congregational Freedom: The Spirit's Presence and the Spirit's Power for a New Century Ministry," in *A Past with a Future*, ed. Steven A. Peay (Oak Creek: Congregational Press, 1998), 61-62.

January 1, 2012
Janglz the Clown

If Harry Butman was in the first generation of leaders of our association, and if Arthur Rouner, Jr., is in the second generation, then Jerold Cochran is in the third generation of our leaders. There are many people here in this church today who remember Jerry and Dorothy Cochran. Jerry was a longtime member and a leader in this local church, serving on the executive council and serving as our moderator. One of the reasons Jerry is special to me is that he was the moderator who signed my ordination certificate when I was ordained as a Congregational minister here at Church of the Oaks in June 2000.

But Jerry did a lot more than that. He was a very talented leader and organizer. He led us through an important revision of our bylaws. Because he was in charge of the men's prayer breakfast on Saturday mornings for quite some time, he was my inspiration when I started the prayer breakfast back up again; but unlike me, Jerry could cook very well. He prepared our breakfast on those Saturday mornings right here in the church building. He did not have to bring a meal that his wife had cooked at home, the way that I do.

Those in our church who knew Jerry will remember his brilliant mind, his winning personality, his kind heart, and his wonderful laugh. Considering some of his outside activities, one would expect a wonderful laugh from Jerry. You might not know that Jerry has also worked as a clown, under the name "Janglz." He joined the International Shrine Clown Association in 1975 and rose to the rank of Illustrious Potentate in that organization. The association's Website says that Jerry looks forward to continuing "participating in the joy of being a clown."

Jerry has an outstanding sense of humor, in spite of having gone through a lot in his lifetime, including the death of a child and several years' struggle with his own health issues. In an article in *The Congregationalist*, Jerry's former pastor—Rev. Robert Coates of First Congregational Church in Salt Lake City—was quoted as follows: "In many ways, Jerry Cochran typifies the business personality, thinking in terms of bottom lines, long-range plans, goals, and efficiency. Yet there is more, much more. He also brings a faith shaped by the constant winds of life's joys and tragedies."[267] The last I

---

[267]Robert Coates and Blaine Simons, "Profile—Executive Committee Chairman Jerold R. Cochran," *The Congregationalist*, October/November 1996, 9, in Larson.

heard, Jerry is now perfectly healthy, the cancer and other problems all behind him. He and Dorothy are very happy at their current home in Oregon.

You may be thinking, "That's all well and good, but why is this man from our little church in the tiny village of Del Rey Oaks, California, being described as a leader in our National Association?" Jerry was born in Pocatello, Idaho, and graduated from Idaho State College, where he married the former Dorothy Karpins. A very successful businessman, he eventually retired as purchasing manager for a manufacturing company in Salt Lake City. He was a Mormon, until he decided that he could no longer follow the teachings of the Latter Day Saints. Led to the Congregational church, he exercised his leadership talents in multiple positions of authority within the local church and local public-service organizations, and beyond that on the board of the Congregational Foundation for Theological Studies and finally in the position of chairman of the Executive Committee of our National Association.

Bob Coates, Jerry's former pastor, was again quoted in that article in *The Congregationalist*: "He, like most of us, struggles to maintain a balance between the pragmatic demands of an organization with much diversity and richness in thought and action, and the desire to discern the vision of what God would have us be, here and now and into the future. If, through his leadership of the Executive Committee, he can help us laugh a bit more deeply, staying in touch with the child within us, he will again have earned his clown name of 'Janglz.' He will lighten our hearts as we search diligently and creatively to find God's way for us and our Association."[268]

---

[268]Ibid.

January 15, 2012
What Is a Congregational Church?

What is a Congregational church? Since we believe in the autonomy and the freedom of the local church, no two Congregational churches are exactly the same. However, based on our beginnings and our continuing tradition, we can make a few generalizations.

A Congregational church is "a gathered church." Congregationalists often turn to Matthew 18:20—"For where two or three are gathered together in My Name, there am I in the midst of them." Each local church is a people who have been gathered together by Jesus Himself, and the Lord Jesus alone is the Head of the church. We have no other authority over us, although we seek fellowship and advice from other churches of like faith and order.

A Congregational church is ruled by the congregation. Government of the local church is not vested in any one person—neither the pastor nor the moderator nor any other single person—but church government is the responsibility of the whole congregation, even if the people have delegated some of their authority to a moderator or to an executive council.

A Congregational church is an orthodox, Trinitarian church. While our polity is distinctive, our theology generally is similar to that of other churches in the Reformed tradition.

A Congregational church attempts to be a true church in the sense that all its members are genuine believers, insofar as that can be determined by mere human beings. Ideally, a person gives a credible testimony to being born again before becoming a church member.

A Congregational church will ordinarily have a pastor who is a Congregationalist, ideally someone who has been raised up from that local congregation. While a Congregational church is free to ordain anyone, our tradition favors pastors who are educated.

A Congregational church listens to the Holy Spirit. In its ideal form, a Congregational church meeting makes no decision until the church is unanimous, having sought the Holy Spirit's guidance. Arthur Rouner, Jr., wrote, "Where the Spirit has led, we have been free to follow."[269]

A Congregational church is a covenant church. Each church creates a church covenant after much deliberation and much prayer, and members periodically affirm that covenant, which is understood to be a solemn

---

[269]Rouner, *Congregational Way*, 80.

agreement among the people, and between the people and God. As John Robinson said, "A company, consisting though of but two or three, separated from the world, and gathered into the name of Christ by a covenant, is a church, and so has the whole power of Christ."[270]

A Congregational church is in fellowship with all other true churches, regardless of their denominational labels. We are truly ecumenically-minded. We believe that each local church that is true to the Gospel is a complete manifestation of the one holy, catholic, and apostolic Church.

A Congregational church is focused on missions. We were involved in the very beginning of the missions movement in America, and we believe in spreading the Gospel to the ends of the earth.

A Congregational church understands that Christians must follow Jesus' admonition that we are to feed the hungry, clothe the naked, and house the homeless.

A Congregational church tends not to be an overly formal church. Vestments and liturgy were abandoned by early Congregationalists. The great John Milton, criticizing the ritual of the Church of England, described "this liturgy, all over in conception lean and dry; of affections empty and unmoving; of passion, or any height whereto the soul might soar upon the wings of zeal, empty and barren."[271]

A Congregational church is characterized by joy and by love. We rejoice in our salvation, and we seek to spread that joy to others. We do our best to love the Lord our God with all our heart, all our soul, all our mind, and all our strength; and to love our neighbor as we love ourselves.

---

[270]Von Rohr, 18.

[271]John Milton, *Complete Poetry and Selected Prose* (New York: The Modern Library, 1950), 602.

About the Author

Robert Hellam was born in 1947 in Carmel, California, in the fifth generation of his family to live on the Monterey Peninsula. He lives in Seaside, California, with his wife, the former Constance Cristobal. Connie and Bob grew up in Seaside, and they have known each other since age three. They have two sons: Chuck, who is a staff sergeant in the U.S. Army and has been in Iraq three times; and Brian, who lives in Sacramento with his wife, Elize. Chuck and his wife, Claire, live in Hawaii with their two daughters, Malia and Leinani. (At this writing, Chuck is deployed to Afghanistan.) Bob, a retired Federal employee, is a teacher at Monterey Bay Christian School in Seaside, and Connie teaches at the same school. Bob is also Associate Pastor at Church of the Oaks in Del Rey Oaks, California. In addition, he is a chaplain (first lieutenant) with the California State Military Reserve (with prior active duty in the U.S. Navy). Bob earned his BA in English and his teaching credential from San José State University, his master of divinity degree from Western Seminary, and the doctor of ministry degree from Trinity Theological Seminary. Bob is a member of the Monterey Bay Colony of the Society of Mayflower Descendants, the Nims Family Association, the Plapp Family Association, American Legion Post 591, and the State Guard Association of the United States.

Other Books by Robert Hellam

Sonnets of David, Book I: A Poetic Paraphrase of Psalms 1-41 (Writers Club Press).

Sonnets of David 2: Books II-III: A Poetic Paraphrase of Psalms 42-89 (Writers Club Press).

Sonnets of David 3: Books IV-V: A Poetic Paraphrase of Psalms 90-150 (iUniverse).

Witnesses of the Nativity (Blurb.com).

"Some New Thing": Paul and the Philosophers: Paul's Epistemology and the Postmodern Impasse (CreateSpace).

(All these books are available through Amazon.com, except Witnesses of the Nativity, *which must be ordered from the publisher, Blurb.com.)*

Bibliography

Ahlstrom, Sydney E. *A Religious History of the American People.* New Haven: Yale University Press, 1972.

Anderson, Jan, ed. *Of People: Literature.* 4th ed. Pensacola: A Beka Books, 2008.

Angle, Paul M., ed. *By These Words: Great Documents of American Liberty, Selected and Placed in Their Contemporary Settings.* San Francisco: Rand McNally & Company, 1954.

Atkins, Gaius Glenn, and Helen E. Phillips. *An Adventure in Liberty: A Short History of the Congregational Christian Churches.* Oak Creek: National Association of Congregational Christian Churches, 1990.

Beecher, Henry Ward. *A Treasury of Illustration*, eds. John R. Howard and Truman J. Ellinwood. New York: Fleming H. Revell Company, 1904. «http://www.ebooksread.com/authors-eng/henry-ward-beecher/a-treasury-of-illustration-cee/» (accessed 29 Apr 2012).

Burbank, Rex, and Jack B. Moore, eds. *The Literature of the American Renaissance.* Columbus: Charles E. Merrill Publishing Company, 1969.

Butman, Harry R. *The Lord's Free People.* Oak Creek: Congregational Press, no date.

_____. *Symbols of Our Way: A Short List of Significant Congregational Statements 1567-1975.* Oak Creek: Congregational Press, no date.

Caffrey, Kate. *The Mayflower.* New York: Stein and Day, 1974.

Carson, Clarence B. *A Basic History of the United States.* 6 vols. Wadley: American Textbook Committee, 1983-96.

Carson, John. "The Congregational Way of Life." *The Congregationalist*, September 2010, 20-22.

Channing, William E. *Works.* 11th ed. Vol. 5. Boston: George G. Channing, 1849.

"Christmas a Crime." *Celebrate Boston.* «http://www.celebrateboston.com/crime/puritan-christmas-law.htm» (accessed 27 Apr 2012).

DeMar, Gary, ed. *Passing the Torch of Liberty to a New Generation.* Powder Springs: American Vision Press, 2009.

Dexter, Henry M. *Congregationalism, What It Is, Whence It Is, How It Works, Why It Is Better Than Any Other Form of Church Government, and Its Consequent Demands.* Boston: Nichols and Noyes, 1865. «http://books.google.com» (accessed 29 Apr 2012).

_____. *A Hand-book of Congregationalism.* Boston: Congregational Publishing Society, 1880. « http://www.kobobooks.com/ebook/A-handbook-of-Congregationalism/book-ZWoIayRr4kqyuLJF9XO0Mg/page1.html» (accessed 29 Apr 2012).

Dixon, Richard Watson. *History of the Church of England.* Oxford: Clarendon Press, 1902). «http://books.google.com/books» (accessed 23 Apr 2012).

Edwards, Jonathan. *The Works of President Edwards.* New York: G. & C. & H. Carvill, 1830. Vol. 4. «http://books.google.com» (accessed 28 Apr 2012).

_____. *A Jonathan Edwards Reader.* Edited by John E. Smith, Harry S. Stout, and Kenneth P. Minkema. New Haven: Yale University Press, 1995.

"Edward Taylor." Answers.com « http://www.answers.com/topic/teddy-taylor» (accessed 28 Apr 2012).

Elwell, Walter A., ed. *Evangelical Dictionary of Theology.* Grand Rapids: Baker Books, 1984.

Federer, William Joseph. *America's God and Country: Encyclopedia of Quotations.* St. Louis: Amerisearch, 2000. «http://books.google.com» (accessed 28 Apr 2012).

Forsyth, P. T. *The Work of Christ.* Blackwood: New Creation Publications, 1994. «www.newcreation.org.au/books/pdf/277_WorkOfChrist.pdf» (accessed 29 Apr 2012).

_____. *The Soul of Prayer.* Blackwood: New Creation Publications, 1999. «www.newcreation.org.au/books/pdf/331_SoulPrayer.pdf» (accessed 29 Apr 2012).

_____. *The Principle of Authority.* Blackwood: New Creation Publications, 2004. «http://www.newcreation.org.au/books/pdf/397_Principle_of_Authority.pdf» (accessed 29 Apr 2012).

Fullard-Leo, Betty. "The Woman Who Changed a Kingdom." *Coffee Times*, June 1998 « www.coffeetimes.com/july98.htm» (accessed 29 Apr 2012).

_____. "Henry Opukaha'ia, the Youth Who Changed Hawaii." *Coffee Times*, Fall 1998 «http://www.coffeetimes.com/henry.htm» (accessed 28 Apr 2012).

González, Justo. *The Story of Christianity.* 2 vols. San Francisco: HarperSanFrancisco, 1984-85.

"Got Questions Ministries." «http://www.gotquestions.org/congregationalism.html» (accessed 29 Apr 2012).

Hartley, Rick. Unpublished lecture notes, Congregational History and Polity Seminar, Boston, July 2011.

Hellam, Robert. "Richard Overton, Prophet of Freedom." *The St. Croix Review* 23, no. 2 (April 1990): 54-61.

Hughes, Raymond F. *The Mayflower Story.* Plymouth: General Society of Mayflower Descendants, 1973.

"International Congregational Fellowship." «http://www.intercong.org/about-us/history/» (accessed 29 Apr 2012).

Larson, Arlin T., ed. *Readings in the History and Polity of the National Association of Congregational Christian Churches.* Demorest: Piedmont College, 1997.

Lindsey, Esther H. *Signers of the Compact Who Left Descendants*. Carmel: Monterey Bay Colony, Society of Mayflower Descendants in the State of California, 1996.

Marshall, Peter J., Jr., and David B. Manuel, Jr. *The Light and the Glory*. Grand Rapids: Fleming H. Revell, 1977.

_____. *From Sea to Shining Sea*. Grand Rapids: Fleming H. Revell, 1986.

_____. *Sounding Forth the Trumpet*. Grand Rapids: Fleming H. Revell, 1999.

McGrath, Alister E., ed. *The Christian Theology Reader*. 2nd ed. Malden: Blackwell Publishing, 2001.

McManners, John, ed. *The Oxford Illustrated History of Christianity*. New York: Oxford University Press, 1992.

Mickus, Kelly Dobbs, ed. *Hymns for a Pilgrim People*. Oak Creek: Congregational Press, 2007.

Milton, John. *Complete Poetry and Selected Prose*. New York: The Modern Library, 1950.

Peay, Steven A., ed. *A Past with a Future*. Oak Creek: Congregational Press, 1998.

_____ and Lloyd M. Hall, Jr., eds. *The 1954 Polity and Unity Report*. Oak Creek: Congregational Press, 2001.

Philbrick, Nathaniel. *Mayflower: A Story of Courage, Community, and War*. New York: Viking, 2006.

"Pilgrim Center for Reconciliation." «http://www.razoo.com/story/Pilgrim-Center-For-Reconciliation» (accessed 29 Apr 2012).

"Poets of Cambridge, U.S.A." «http://www.harvardsquarelibrary.org/poets/taylor.php» (accessed 28 Apr 2012).

Rauschenbusch, Walter. *A Theology for the Social Gospel*. New York: The Macmillan Company, 1917.

Rouner, Arthur, Jr., *The Congregational Way of Life*. Oak Creek: Congregational Press, 1972.

Sawyer, M. James. *Biographies of Theologians Significant in Doctrinal Development*. San Jose: By the author, 1996.

Schaff, Philip, ed. *The Creeds of Christendom*. 3 vols. Grand Rapids: Baker Book House, 1990.

Sheldon, Charles M. *In His Steps*. New York: Grosset & Dunlap, 1935.

Sherman, Robert M., ed. *Mayflower Families through Five Generations*. Plymouth: General Society of Mayflower Descendants, 1978.

Simons, M. Laird. "Dwight Lyman Moody." *Wholesome Words: Christian Biography Resources*. «www.wholesomewords.org/biography/biomoody.html» (accessed 4 September 2011).

Smith, E. Brooks, and Robert Meredith, eds. *Pilgrim Courage: From a Firsthand Account by William Bradford, Governor of Plymouth Colony: Selected Episodes from His Original History* Of Plimoth

Plantation: *And Passages from the Journals of William Bradford and Edward Winslow*. Boston: Little, Brown and Company, 1962.

Swift, Lindsay Swift. *The Massachusetts Election Sermons*. Cambridge: John Wilson and Son, 1897. «http://www.archive.org/stream/massachusettsele00swif/massachusett sele00swif_djvu.txt» (accessed 28 Apr 2012).

Van Doren, Charles, and Robert McHenry, eds. *Webster's Guide to American History*. Springfield: G. & C. Merriam Company, 1971.

Von Rohr, John. *The Shaping of American Congregationalism 1620-1957*. Cleveland: The Pilgrim Press, 1992.

Waddington, John. *Congregational History 1200-1567*. London: Longmans, Green, & Co., 1869. «http://www.archive.org/stream/congregationalhi1869wadd/congregat ionalhi1869wadd_djvu.txt» (accessed 24 Apr 2012).

_____. *Congregational History, 1700-1800*. London: Longmans, Green, and Co., 1874. «http://www.ebooksread.com/authors-eng/john-waddington/congregational-history-1700-1800-in-relation-to-contemporaneous-events-educat-hci/1-congregational-history-1700-1800-in-relation-to-contemporaneous-events-educat-hci.shtml» (accessed 23 Apr 2012).

Walker, Williston, ed. *The Creeds and Platforms of Congregationalism*. New York: The Pilgrim Press, 1991.

"Washington Gladden Society." «http://washingtongladdensociety.org/about.html» (accessed 29 Apr 2012).

When Christmas Was Banned in Boston," *Massachusetts Travel Journal*. «http://masstraveljournal.com/comment/116» (accessed 27 Apr 2012).

Wicker, Les, and Rick Hartley. "The Christian Connexion," *The Congregationalist*, December 2009, 14-16, 21.

Willison, George F. *Saints and Strangers: Being the Lives of the Pilgrim Fathers & Their Families, with Their Friends & Foes; & an Account of Their Posthumous Wanderings in Limbo, Their Final Resurrection & Rise to Glory, & the Strange Pilgrimages of Plymouth Rock*. New York: Reynal & Hitchcock, 1945.

Wolfe, Don M., ed. *Leveller Manifestoes of the Puritan Revolution*. New York: Humanities Press, 1967.

Young, Carlton R., ed. *The Book of Hymns*. Nashville: The United Methodist Publishing House, 1966.

"Zabdiel Boylston," *Today in Science History*. «http://todayinsci.com/B/Boylston_Zabdiel/Boylston_Zabdiel.htm» (accessed 28 Apr 2012).

"Zabdiel Boylston," *Celebrate Boston*. «http://www.celebrateboston.com/biography/zabdiel-boylston.htm» (accessed 28 Apr 2012).

Made in the USA
Coppell, TX
13 October 2021

63979144R00085